CW00671133

The Troublesome Priest

A PRAYER FOR THE GRANTING OF
A JUST PRIEST
by Bishop Thomas Ken
(Bishop of Bath and Wells 1685–91)

Give me the priest these graces shall possess;
Of an ambassador the just address,
A father's tenderness, a shepherd's care,
A leader's courage, which the cross can bear,
A ruler's arm, a watchman's wakeful eye,
A pilot's skill, the helm in storms to ply,
A fisher's patience and a lab'rer's toil.
A guide's dexterity to disembroil,
A prophet's inspiration from above.
A teacher's knowledge, and a Saviour's love.
Give me the priest, a light upon the hill,
Whose rays his whole circumference can fill;
In God's own word and sacred learning vers'd,
Deep in the study of the heart immers'd.

Also by Jonathan Tucker

THE SILK ROAD: ART AND HISTORY

The Troublesome Priest

HAROLD DAVIDSON
RECTOR OF STIFFKEY

———

Jonathan Tucker

MICHAEL RUSSELL

First published in Great Britain 2007
by Michael Russell (Publishing) Ltd
Wilby Hall, Wilby, Norwich NR16 2JP

Page makeup in Sabon by Waveney Typesetters
Wymondham, Norfolk
Printed and bound in Great Britain
by Biddles Ltd, King's Lynn, Norfolk

ISBN 978-0-85955-307-0

FOR GRACE OLIVIA JANE TUCKER

Contents

	Acknowledgements	ix
	Author's Note	xi
	Family Tree	xiii
1	Background and Early Life	1
2	Extra-Parochial Activities	13
3	Trouble Ahead	20
4	The Trial Begins	42
5	The Rector Takes the Stand	72
6	Verdict	101
7	Hell Hath No Fury Like a Parson Scorned	113
8	Cleric in a Cask	127
9	Harold Davidson's Last Adventure	139
10	Was Davidson Guilty?	152
11	Loose Ends	160
	Bibliography	171
	Index	173

Acknowledgements

I should like to express my particular thanks to the following people, all of whom either helped to get this project off the ground or made possible its completion: Michael Russell for his publisher's eye; our good friend Ned Hamond, son of Major Philip Hamond, who first sparked my interest in the story of Harold Davidson; my wife Antonia Tozer – for her forbearance, for her photographic skills and for listening politely to 'just one more' tale about the rector; Dick Meadows of the BBC, who has been a great source of information, ideas and photographs relating to the rector's life; Harold Davidson's grandson Colin St Johnston, son of his eldest child Sheilagh – he provided a wealth of information about the family's reaction to the events of 1932 and filled in some of the many gaps in this story; Mrs Francis Pierce at the *Eastern Daily Press* Library for her kind assistance with scanning large numbers of newspaper cuttings relating to the Davidson affair; Tony Sharkey, a local Blackpool historian, for some fascinating background material about promenade sideshows and for information about Davidson's activities in the town between 1932 and 1936; Cyril Critchlow, former owner of a museum of Blackpool history, for providing information about the impresario Luke Gannon; Ron Severs for his knowledge of 1930s Blackpool and for supplying some of the postcards printed by Harold Davidson in support of his cause; Mrs Betty Lucas, daughter of Captain Rye, for her stories about promenade life in 1930s Skegness and for providing information about the last months of the rector's life; the Revd John Penny, the recently retired incumbent of Stiffkey; David Haviland, David Smith and Susan Hazeldine for reading through the manuscript, for offering many helpful suggestions and for being merciful in their criticisms; Ms Dawn Bradley at the Skegness Library for information about both the rector and 1930s Skegness; the staff at the National Archives, Kew, the Norfolk Record Office and the Lambeth Palace Library.

I am also much indebted to the late Tom Cullen, author of *The Prostitutes' Padre*, his account of the Davidson affair, for recording the evidence of many of the key protagonists while they were still alive.

PHOTOGRAPHIC ACKNOWLEDGEMENTS

Ned Hamond, 7; Betty Lucas, 24, 25, 26, 27, 30; Dick Meadows, 9, 21, 28; Colin St Johnston, 1, 2; Topix, 10, 23; Antonia Tozer, 13, 29; Anna White, 6.

Author's Note

Tom Cullen's book, *The Prostitutes' Padre*, is a mine of information about the Davidson affair in general and his character in particular. Cullen was fortunate that many of the key players in this strange tale were still alive while he was researching the book in the early 1970s. Harold Davidson's family and many of Stiffkey's villagers were enraged by Cullen's account – they believed that it traduced the name of a man who had done no wrong. Even some thirty years later, during the research for this biography, many of the rector's supporters referred dismissively to 'that book'. The debate over Harold Davidson's guilt or innocence is as intense as ever among those who knew him and those who have an interest in the events of 1932. Cullen's book may have its flaws – there is perhaps a little too much psychobabble in his account – but much of what he wrote is borne out by my own research and he is especially good on the subject of Harold Davidson's character.

Cullen's attempt to explain Davidson's behaviour includes one theme that recurs throughout his book. I repeat it here, and then leave it to the reader to accept or reject it. Cullen repeatedly refers to Davidson as suffering from a multiple (or dissociated) personality disorder, defined in the *New Oxford Dictionary of English* as 'a rare dissociative disorder in which two or more personalities with distinct memories and behaviour patterns apparently exist in one individual'.

This explanation was first suggested by J. Rowland Sales, Davidson's press agent, who felt that Davidson had three distinct personalities, between which he alternated at different times. The first Sales called 'Uncle Harold', the amiable and well-intentioned village priest adored by his congregation. The second personality Sales called 'Little Jimmy' – which was, in fact, the affectionate sobriquet given to the 5ft 3in Davidson by his parishioners. Sales applied the name in a different sense, referring to a mischievous self-destructive side to Davidson's character. The third personality Sales called the 'Bunco Kid', named after the American slang word for swindler or grifter. This seldom revealed itself, according to Sales, but there were instances, recounted later in this book, when it did.

To illustrate his theory Sales cited an incident that occurred in a Lyons teashop in London. He was sitting with Davidson and listening to a story about an elderly couple whom Davidson had discovered sleeping under a hedge. It transpired that they had been evicted from their tied cottage and left homeless. Davidson had given the couple shelter and fed them. He was visibly upset as he told Sales the story, caring and concerned. Then a new 'nippy' waitress came by and his demeanour abruptly changed. Suddenly he was 'Little Jimmy'– at his most oleaginous. 'Excuse me, Miss,' he said to the girl, 'you must be the sister of Jessie Matthews [then a theatrical star].' He leapt up and, abandoning the startled Sales, rushed out of the teashop, promising the equally startled waitress that he would get her a part in a new play that was about to open in London.

Sales thought that the Church mishandled the Davidson affair. Rather than charging Davidson with offences of immorality, what the Church ought to have done was to offer Davidson a prolonged course of psychotherapy. At the trial, Sales tells us, 'An expression of amazed disbelief would cross Uncle Harold's face as Little Jimmy's escapades were ascribed to him.' That evidence certainly does no harm to Sales's theory that Davidson was suffering from a multiple personality disorder.

Probably no one, however, would have been better qualified to comment on Davidson's complexities than his wife Molly, or 'Mimi' as the family called her. At the conclusion of his trial in 1932 she granted an interview to the *Sunday Dispatch* in which she makes some extremely illuminating remarks about his character. She and 'Paddy' (Patricia), the Davidsons' third child, talked about the effects of the case on the family and about what they considered to have been the injustice of it all. The interview is examined on pages 109–11.

KEY MEMBERS OF THE DAVIDSON FAMILY
REFERRED TO IN THIS STORY

Revd Francis Davidson, b. 1837
m. 1874 Alice Selina Augusta Hodgskin, b. 1853

Harold Francis, b. 14 July 1875, d. 30 July 1937
m. 1906 Moyra (Molly) Cassandra Saurin

Muriel Alice b.1883
m. Bertie Cox

Sheilagh	Nugent	Patricia	Arnold	Pamela
b. 1907	b. 1909	b. 1911	b. 1914	b. 1919

Background and Early Life

Harold Davidson was born on 14 July 1875 in the unappealing Southampton suburb of Sholing, the first of two children. His father, the Revd Francis Davidson (b. 1837), had been vicar of St Mary's Church, Sholing since 1866. Short in stature but pugnacious when the occasion demanded it, he displayed great compassion to the most needy of his parishioners and served them faithfully and without a blemish to his name for forty-eight years. An extraordinary twenty-seven members of the Davidson family are claimed to have joined the clergy and it was never doubted that Harold would follow suit. On her side of the family, Harold's mother Alice, as the great-niece of Arnold of Rugby, had her own good moral pedigree. But the parish was a poor backwater and the family's circumstances were progressively straitened, particularly as Alice Davidson suffered from almost permanent ill health after the birth of her daughter, Muriel Alice, in 1883.

At six, Harold attended the Banister Court School in Southampton, established originally for the sons of officers of the P&O shipping line. Two of his contemporaries were J. Maundy Gregory, later notorious for the sale of political honours during Lloyd George's premiership, and Ernest Doudemain (sometimes Du Domaine), later putative father of the fifth Davidson child. Davidson himself stayed at Banister Court only until 1890, when he was placed in the care of his mother's two unmarried sisters, Gertrude and Mary Hodgskin, and sent to the Whitgift School in Croydon. Here he performed poorly, confounding his father's hopes that he would win a scholarship to study theology at university. However, through the influence of Aunt Gertrude he carried out volunteer work in London's East End, which evidently saw the beginnings of his Socialist leanings. He became involved with both Toynbee Hall and the Fabian Society. Toynbee Hall was established in the East End in 1884 to commemorate the life and work of the social reformer Arnold Toynbee, who had died the previous year. Samuel Barnett, canon of St Jude's Church, Whitechapel, ran it with his wife

Henrietta. The idea was to create a place where graduates from Oxford and Cambridge could live and work among the poor. They could provide practical help and inspiration to the disadvantaged and, at the same time, develop social consciences that would influence and sustain them during their subsequent professional lives. Clement Attlee, the Labour prime minister, and William Beveridge, one of the creators of the Welfare State, were both residents at one time, and the left of centre think tank, the Fabian Society, drew many of its early members from Toynbee Hall.

It was at Whitgift that Davidson's interest in the theatre began, prompted by one of his classmates, Leon Quartermaine, who was to make his career as an actor on both stage and screen. (Among his credits is as Jacques in J. M. Barrie's 1936 adaptation of *As You Like It*, which featured Laurence Olivier as Orlando and Elisabeth Bergner, delivering some of her lines in a very precarious English accent, as Rosalind. The piece was directed by her husband, Paul Czinner.) Davidson and Quartermaine spent their summer holidays organising theatre performances around Sholing, sometimes on the vicarage lawn. Just before Davidson left Whitgift he appeared with Quartermaine in a comedy called *Sent to the Tower* – playing a pastry cook – and within a few months of leaving school he was on the stage in London, performing a comedy routine at the Steinway Hall in Lower Seymour Street. His genre was that of the 'drawing room entertainer', a gentle form of light comedy popular at the time. Davidson did not become a star but he did do passably well in touring productions in the provinces, particularly as Charley's Aunt in the farce of that name which, first produced in London in 1892, is about young courting couples and the chaperone system. Davidson's role was that of Lord Fancourt Babberley, masquerading as the wealthy aunt from Brazil ('where the nuts come from'). It was not an occupation his father would have chosen for him.

There was very much another side, however, to the young Davidson. His early life was upright and austere. According to his grandson Colin St Johnston,[1] he joined the Temperance Society at the age of sixteen and abstained from alcohol throughout his life. Conscious that his true calling was the Church, he is also said to have made a point of visiting the local elderly during touring productions and reading to them from the

[1] Interview with the author, 19 April 2004.

Bible. And then there was the incident in November 1894, a sort of epiphany. He describes it in *The Reason Why*, a pamphlet he published in 1934:

> I was walking along the Thames Embankment in a very thick London fog thirty-nine years ago last November when I was lucky enough to rescue a girl of 16½ years old who had tried to jump into the river for the purpose of self-destruction. She turned out to be a girl who had run away from her home in a little village near Cambridge ten days before, hoping to get a job of work in London, and had met with tragically unhappy experiences, after the money she had brought away from home with her was spent... [she was] stranded on the London streets. Her pitiful story made a tremendous impression on me... After sending her back home with a letter to her mother... I have ever since, whenever I had any spare time in town, kept my eyes open for opportunities to help that type of girl, namely, the country girl stranded on the alluring streets of London, of which there is an enormous number every year.

In the autumn of 1898 Davidson entered Exeter College, Oxford, to study for the priesthood. His entry was facilitated by the Revd Basil Wilberforce, himself an alumnus of Exeter and a friend of the Davidson family. Wilberforce, son of the Bishop of Oxford and chaplain to the House of Commons, was also a champion of teetotalism and clearly Davidson's espousal of the cause was at the root of their association.

Davidson's time at Oxford appears to have been undistinguished and fairly uneventful. He was short of funds and had to continue his theatrical career to support himself. Because he was self-financing he took considerably longer than usual to complete his degree (five years instead of three), finally graduating in June 1903, having been told to remove himself from Exeter in March 1901 and completing his time at Grindle's Hall, an Oxford forcing establishment. He failed many of his exams because of his lifelong habit of being late for everything, but somehow managed to muddle through. He was blessed with a phenomenal memory and was an excellent chess-player, becoming president of the Oxford University Chess Club and captaining a joint Oxford-Cambridge chess team that defeated an American universities side. The match was played via a transatlantic radio link, the first of its kind.

Some details of Davidson's life at Oxford are contained in the auto-biography of his friend (Sir) Reginald Kennedy-Cox, the renowned philanthropist, social reformer and founder of the Dockland Settlements organisations, who remembered Davidson as a brilliant man with boundless energy. He provides a startling appraisal of his friend (even though he does not actually name him):

There was one brilliant little man who was amongst my intimate friends, and who is quite the most provocative character I have ever met. By all the rules of life he should be today a man of authority and outstanding success, but he is a failure, I fear, and always will be. He dreams continuously of the days when he is really going to do big things, but these days never come. I have seldom known a man with such relentless driving force, and so oblivious of fatigue, but his assets are stultified by perpetual unpunctuality and a complete lack of a sense of proportion. He is now a vicar in a remote Norfolk living. When he was up at the Varsity he did the oddest things. Once he insisted on interviewing the Vice-Chancellor in bed. It was over quite a trivial matter, one of no urgency whatever. The Vice-Chancellor was racked with the excruciating pains of gout, quite the wrong time to interview him, but with his usual ill-chosen judgement my friend slipped by the Vice-Chancellor's butler and ran up to the invalid's room.

Again, he was often ploughed in his exams, because he was always late, but he would insist upon ending his half-finished examination papers with an elaborate and detailed invitation to his examiners to come to tea with him in his rooms, when they would be able to satisfy themselves as to his knowledge upon the subjects which he had been much too late to tackle. This oddity of life continued, and does so up to this very day. When he came to London, after being ordained, he loved to find his way behind the scenes in nearly every London theatre, and, as always, indifferent to all rules and regulations, he would force an entry right on to the stage. One would view from the audience the puzzling spectacle of a clearly defined and rather odd clerical shadow reflected by strong limelight, and marring perhaps a particularly beautiful scene. Only the other day he told me less in sorrow than with interest that he believed that he is the only officer in the Great War

who got a consistent 'bad report' from all his commanding officers. And yet, with it all, here is a man with a heart of gold,
outstanding ability, boundless energy and overwhelming sympathy. What could not he have done if only he had self-discipline as
well? In spite of his shortcomings he did much, I believe, to shape
my life. In his company I met all sorts and conditions of men. My
first real helper down at the Docks was the result of his introduc-
tion, and I remember, most important of all, that I registered a
solemn vow what I would never flutter about, as he undoubtedly
did, but would concentrate upon some particular job and stick to
it for all I was worth.[2]

Kennedy-Cox was called as a defence witness at Davidson's trial. He
described his old friend as 'quite the most eccentric man I have ever
met'.

The other key event to occur in Davidson's life during his time at
Oxford was that the theatre troupe of Miss Annie Horniman (of Horniman's Tea fame) came to town. One of its members was a young, spir-
ited and beautiful actress called Moyra Cassandra Saurin. Davidson
was captivated by Molly, as she was known – early photographs reveal
that she was a blonde, blue-eyed beauty.[3] They fell in love and became
engaged in 1901 but their relationship was turbulent, to say the least.
Molly was a strong-willed Irishwoman from a comfortably off
landowning family, from Garballagh, near Duleek, County Meath and
was not afraid to express her opinions. It was five years before they
finally married, on 9 October 1906, and their engagement was almost
broken off on several occasions.

Davidson had failed both his intermediate and final examinations on
the first attempt, and the Bishop of Oxford was initially reluctant to
ordain him into the priesthood. But eventually Davidson made it
through and was ordained as a curate at Holy Trinity Church, Windsor,
with a secondary duty as assistant chaplain to the Household Cavalry

---

2 Reginald Kennedy-Cox, *An Autobiography*, London: Hodder and Stoughton,
1931.
3 The photograph of Molly (illustration 1) is interesting in a number of respects.
It was taken in 1910 when she was presented as a 'Matron' at the Court of St
James. According to her grandson Colin St Johnston, the bouquet of flowers is
strategically placed to conceal the fact that she was pregnant with her third child,
Patricia.

at Combermere Barracks. His time at Windsor was short and appears
to have aroused little controversy but he does appear to have made a
few enemies. Among the voluminous correspondence sent to Major
Philip Hamond after 'The Kick' of 21 August 1932 (see pages 119–20),
there is a letter from one W. E. Mason of Windsor, an estate agent and
clearly no friend of Davidson:

> I had the misfortune, some years ago, of knowing Harold David-
> son when he was a curate in this town & felt I must write to
> congratulate you on kicking his posterior. I expect at the time you
> felt it was worth at least £5.
>
> Yours faithfully,
> W. E. MASON[4]

In 1905, after only two years at Windsor, Davidson was sent to be
the assistant curate at St Martin-in-the Fields in Central London. He
was there for only a year, being appointed in May 1906 as rector of the
village of Stiffkey (with Morston) on the North Norfolk coast, a living
in the gift of the Townshend family of Raynham. When later that same
year, in October, he married Molly, the couple returned from honey-
moon in Paris to his new post.

Charles Townshend, the 2nd Viscount (1675–1738), was Secretary
of State to George I and subsequently served as Lord Lieutenant of
Ireland and President of the Privy Council. He is still remembered by
his nickname 'Turnip Townshend' for his development of crop rota-
tion. His descendant John James Dudley Stuart Townshend, the 6th
Marquess (1866–1921), came to the attention of the public for somewhat less wholesome reasons. Davidson was acquainted with a
Yorkshire businessman of rather dubious repute called Thomas
Sutherst. Around 1905 Sutherst's daughter, Gladys Ethel Gwendolen
Eugenie Sutherst, set her cap on marrying Lord Townshend, despite
the fact that he was twenty years older than her, owned very little land
and appears to have been somewhat unstable. He is also said to have
had an affair with his male estate manager. Townshend was all for the
idea, believing that he was marrying the daughter of a millionaire and
not (which was the reality) a bankrupt with over a quarter of a million
pounds of debts. Townshend's relations threatened to have him

4 Letter to Major Philip Hamond dated 15 October 1932.

certified[5] if he married Gladys but he was undeterred. On 9 August 1905 the couple were married at St Martin-in-the-Fields in London – by Harold Davidson.

Townshend rewarded Davidson with the benefice of Stiffkey with Morston, a living worth £503 per annum and increased to £800 during Davidson's incumbency. There was a fine Georgian rectory and sixty acres of glebe land. Davidson was expected to serve the parish only on Saturdays and Sundays, leaving him free to live in London during the week. His £800 salary was double the average vicar's wage at the time.

According to the *Dictionary of English Place-Names* Stiffkey, in Old English, means 'island, or dry ground in marsh, with tree-stumps'. Stiffkey village is now a thriving holiday and weekend destination with a popular pub called The Red Lion, a general store and a couple of antique shops much frequented by affluent Londoners. Property values all along this stretch of coast are bounding along and many of the cottages that were occupied by farm workers in Davidson's day are now weekend retreats for Southerners. The area has become cosmopolitan and a magnet for weekend visitors – Burnham Market, a few miles to the west of Stiffkey, is the epicentre of all this activity and has been nicknamed 'Chelsea-on-Sea' by local people. The whole area is compellingly beautiful and, even today, steeped in age and slightly mysterious. Harold Davidson would now be hard pressed to recognise the village that he knew – even the vicarage no longer belongs to the Church; it is now a private residence. In his day Stiffkey was a remote, impoverished place with a population (according to the 1931 Census) of 356. The villagers supported themselves principally by farming and by the gathering of cockles, known as 'Stewkey Blues'. (The locals, incidentally, seem not to subscribe to the view that Stiffkey should be pronounced 'Stewkey'.) Today, in July and August, there are ceaseless convoys of cars and caravans passing through the village – something of a hazard to pedestrians as the main road has no pavements.

---

5 In August 1906 Lord Townshend's sanity was indeed examined by a judicial hearing. It found him to be sane but incapable of managing his own affairs, although the legality of the marriage was not affected. Townshend, who died in 1921, was an avid collector of clocks. Gladys survived until 1959, serving as Lady Mayoress of King's Lynn and president of the Royal Norfolk Agricultural Association. Her father died aboard the *Lusitania* when it was torpedoed by the Germans in May 1915. Lady Townshend acted as witness at the wedding of Davidson and Molly and attended Davidson's funeral.

There is a wealth of information about life in Stiffkey during the first decades of the twentieth century in Elizabeth Thomas's book *Joe Jordan: Guardian of the Marsh.*[6] Her father was Joe Jordan (1912–2003), a local character who offered his own recollections of the Davidson affair in the 1994 BBC documentary *Matter of Fact.* Joe Jordan's father, Thomas Jordan (d. 1926), was a merchant mariner for many years, who was eventually forced to retire due to ill health. He then worked as a gardener and general handyman for Harold Davidson at the Stiffkey vicarage. Joe Jordan's life was typical of working class families in the village. He was one of thirteen children and, after his father had to give up seafaring, his mother helped to feed them by going to the marshes to gather cockles. The women of the village would venture out, fifteen or twenty to a group, and spend the day scooping up the cockles into wicker baskets carried on their backs. They stayed out in all weathers, dressed in little more than a shawl and a long skirt pinned up between their legs. They would stagger back with their loads at the end of the day and sell them to local cockle-merchants for a few pence. The abject poverty endured by a large proportion – perhaps even a majority – of the population of the North Norfolk coast during this period is an important factor in understanding Davidson's behaviour. Stiffkey's villagers supplemented their meagre incomes by fishing, growing vegetables and gathering shellfish and samphire. There was little money for luxuries but the village did sustain a surprisingly large number of tradesmen and shops. There were three different butchers, three grocery shops, a general shop and no less than three pubs: The Victoria Inn, The Townshend Arms and The Red Lion (which still operates). There was also a blacksmith, a cobbler and a village midwife by the name of Becky, married to a local fisherman, who offered her services for free or for a token glass of gin!

The Stiffkey village school was beside the church and consisted of two rooms, one for infants and the other for juniors. Harold Davidson would visit the school first thing on Monday mornings, presumably just before setting off for London, to sign the register and pray with the children. The school governess was Mrs Grey, wife of Colonel Grey (she features unhappily on page 27). The village children lived on a diet of

6 Elizabeth Thomas, *Joe Jordan: Guardian of the Marsh*, Fakenham, Norfolk: E. M. Thomas, 2003.

bread and margarine with jam or treacle for lunch; and boiled vegetables and perhaps some rabbit or fish for supper. Holidays were unheard of and even simple treats, such as a visit to the annual Wells Regatta or to the circus, were few and far between. Joe Jordan describes the circus animals being driven along the Wells-Cromer road, and the sight of an elephant in a remote village like Stiffkey would have been a major diversion.

Cockling was regarded as women's work and most of the village men were employed on local farms. Farm labourers once occupied the small cottages that now change hands for large sums of money, although in those days a tin bath and an outside privy were the norm. Among the local farms were Vale Farm and several properties owned by the Groom family,[7] for whom Joe Jordan worked for over fifty years. Glebe Farm, which came with the benefice of Stiffkey, was cultivated on Harold Davidson's behalf by a Mr Sam Wordingham. Joe Jordan, like most of his contemporaries, worked part-time from the age of eleven to bring in extra money for the family. As a boy he earned a pound a week during harvest time and then left school at the age of fourteen to tend the sheep that grazed out on the Stiffkey salt marshes. During the long working life that followed he seems to have worked in almost every aspect of farming, from pulling turnips to tending livestock.

Stiffkey village is on an estuary that remained tidal until about the sixteenth century. The village actually comprised two manors, dating at least as far back as the Norman Conquest, and there were also two churches within the same churchyard – St John the Baptist and the now defunct church of St Mary. The two churches existed as separate entities until 1563, when the two were combined and St Mary's was deconsecrated. There were still remains of the old church to be seen until the late nineteenth century and parts of the stained glass windows, still visible in the nave of the surviving church, are thought to be from St Mary's.

Like the community in which it stands, the church of St John the Baptist has acquired additions, alterations and adaptations throughout its lifetime. The earliest parts, most notably the niche on the south side of the chancel, date from the twelfth century or earlier but the First

---

7 Colonel Groom was an implacable adversary of Harold Davidson. See page 113.

World War memorial and the Roll of Honour for the Second remind us that Stiffkey, like almost every village in Britain, paid a price in the twentieth-century conflicts. The people who have left their mark on village history are also in evidence in the church and in its graveyard. The black marble monument to Sir Nathaniel Bacon, the local knight who built Stiffkey Hall in the seventeenth century, is in the chancel. The monument, erected by Bacon himself in 1615, contains the names of many of the principal local families of the time, including some whose descendants were to figure three centuries later in the Davidson affair:

> Nathaniel Bacon 'gilded knight', born the second son of Nicholas Bacon, Lord Keeper of the Great Seal of England, sleeps here in Christ, for whom he was vigilant while alive, with his two dearest wives: Anne, daughter of Thomas Gresham 'gilded knight' and Dorothy, daughter of Arthur Hopton of Wittham, of the same rank. From the former of these he produced three daughters: Anne who married John Townsend of Rainham, Elizabeth who married Thomas Knivet of Ashwellthorp, and Winefred who married Robert Gaudy of Claxton – individuals from the order of knights.
>
> He, mindful of his mortality, and in certain hope of resurrection in Christ, set up this (monument) for himself and his family in his 69th year of our Lord 1615. [Translation of the epitaph of Sir Nathaniel Bacon, extracted from John K. Coleridge, *St John the Baptist Church, Stiffkey, Norfolk: A Guide round the Church*, Church pamphlet, 1993.]

Davidson's grave is beside a small gate on the north side of the churchyard and is still tended by the villagers. A rose bush beside the grave still blooms every summer and there is a new, white marble headstone in the form of a cross with a simple inscription that reads: 'Harold Francis Davidson M.A. Priest, For 26 years Rector of Stiffkey and Morston, Born July 14th 1875, Died July 30th 1937. For on faith in man and genuine love of man all searching after truth must be founded. R.S.' (R.S. is Robert Louis Stevenson and this quotation was also on Davidson's original headstone.)

The headstone faces in the opposite direction to its neighbours. It is tempting to interpret this detail as a metaphor on the rector's approach to life but the truth is more prosaic. A Norfolk clergyman told me that this is a common practice when a cleric is interred – at the Resurrection he will already be facing his flock.

For the well-to-do the nineteenth century was clearly a prosperous era; many of the improvements and additions were made to the church during that period. Stiffkey's beautiful old twenty-room Georgian rectory, built in 1756 and the stage for much of the drama surrounding the Davidson affair, is on the other side of the road from the church and is now a private residence. In Davidson's day it was a meeting place for a succession of weird and wonderful guests, including a host of East End showgirls and waitresses up from London for a spell, a middle aged lady called Mrs Allman recuperating (at the rector's invitation) from influenza; and Ernest Doudemain, who lived at the rectory with his two sons and appears later in this story. During Davidson's time there were often as many as two dozen people staying at the vicarage and, since none of its doors was ever locked, people were constantly stumbling in and out of each other's rooms. Davidson's wife Molly bred angora rabbits, and at one stage the rectory was virtually overrun with them.[8] Davidson's press agent J. Rowland Sales was a regular visitor; he told Cullen that none of the windows had curtains and many were broken, with rags stuffed in the holes to keep out draughts. Amidst all this mayhem, between 1907 and 1913 Davidson and Molly produced four children – Sheilagh, Nugent, Patricia and Arnold. A fifth child, Pamela, was born in 1919.

Molly seems to have heartily disapproved of the endless stream of waifs and strays – invariably young and invariably female – arriving at the door of the rectory. Davidson used to say to her, 'My mission is to help lame dogs over stiles.' Her retort was that 'lame cats' was a more accurate description. She set them to work in the rectory kitchen but never ceased to resent the intrusion, telling him that, 'No man can associate with...the vilest dregs of humanity without getting tar-marked.'[9] Davidson's prime ministerial inspiration, it seems, was William Ewart Gladstone. Gladstone and his wife used to bring prostitutes home to

8 Letter from G. R. Curson to Dick Meadows of the BBC, 27 July 1993. Curson's father, Richard Ernest Curson, was a pallbearer at Davidson's funeral.
9 This quote, and other insights into Davidson's character, are recorded in the interview given by Molly and Patricia to the *Sunday Dispatch* on Sunday 10 July 1932, two days after the conclusion of his trial (see pages 109–11).

rescue them from a life on the streets. No one has seriously questioned Gladstone's motives for helping these women although Roy Jenkins's biography[10] suggests that he experienced a sexual frisson when he came into contact with them.

10 Roy Jenkins, *Gladstone*, London: Macmillan, 1996.

2

Extra-Parochial Activities

It is difficult to estimate how many girls Davidson helped during the thirty-eight years between his first encounter with the girl in the Thames and his trial in 1932. Many were drifting into prostitution to make ends meet (in a manner of speaking), though there were others – like seventeen-year-old Barbara Harris, shortly to enter this story – who rather relished misbehaving. In his pamphlet *The Reason Why* Davidson claims that between 1919 (when he returned from the First World War) and 1934 (when it was written), he helped somewhere between two and three thousand girls:

> …I was picking up in this way roughly, as my diaries show, an average of about 150 to 200 girls a year, and taking them to restaurants[1] for a meal and a talk, and of these I was able definitely to help into good jobs of work a very large number. It is wonderfully interesting and very valuable work, and work that I feel every clergyman should be doing on any opportunity that may occur. It is work that cannot be done discreetly and is attended with a certain amount of risk, but in these days of moral laxity surely no Christian Priest should shirk the opportunity of living dangerously for God. One either does not touch this work at all, or else one must necessarily run the risk of being constantly misunderstood when doing it.

Before the outbreak of the First World War Davidson's early work in London was predominantly with underprivileged boys in the East End. The Newsboys' Club was established principally to improve the lot of the young newsboys who were exploited by Fleet Street and paid a pittance to sell newspapers. They frequently engaged in 'turf battles'. The purpose of the club was to 'safeguard boys living in criminal surroundings', and they were given meals, encouraged to play games

1 By 'restaurants' Davidson probably means modestly priced cafés.

together, and generally steered towards a more stable *modus vivendi*. It was largely through the likes of Davidson that they secured better wages and improvements in their working conditions.

Davidson was also a trustee of his friend Reginald Kennedy-Cox's London Dockland Settlement, recruiting helpers and soliciting funds. He apparently made an enduring mark: Queen Mary, who was later a regular visitor to the Settlement, would reputedly ask Kennedy-Cox how 'our little rector' was getting on. But 'our little rector' had for some time past turned his attention more to delinquents of the other sex. In 1906 he became a chaplain to the Actors' Church Union based at St Paul's Church, Covent Garden, ministering to the spiritual needs of London's showgirls. This was the golden age of music hall entertainment and Davidson, in his element retreading the old theatre haunts of his youth, was often to be found backstage after a performance. In this he seems to have been a little over-zealous and he was barred from a number of theatres after his habit of barging into girls' changing rooms led to complaints. Reginald Kennedy-Cox refers to Davidson's backstage antics in his memoirs. Perhaps there was an inappropriate reason for his behaviour; perhaps it was just that his enthusiasm simply ran away with him.

Beginning in the years immediately before the war Davidson also made frequent trips to Paris. According to Ronald Blythe in his account of the Davidson affair,[2] between 1910 and 1913 the rector went to Paris once a fortnight. A number of the trips were associated with his Actors' Church Union activities, chaperoning newly recruited dancers to the Folies Bergère. At his trial in 1932 Davidson said that he had a friend who ran a school just outside Paris and would also take girls there to work as maids.

In any event, Davidson's weekday routine in London was interrupted by the outbreak of war. He enlisted on 4 October 1915 as an acting chaplain with the Royal Navy. Dissatisfaction with his life at Stiffkey may well have been as persuasive as a patriotic urge to serve his country. His choice of the Royal Navy probably stemmed from the fact that his grandfather and great-grandfather, on his mother's side,

2 Ronald Blythe, *The Age of Illusion: Some Glimpses of Britain Between the Wars, 1919–1940*, Oxford: O.U.P., 1963. The book contains a chapter on the Davidson affair.

served in the Royal Navy during the first half of the nineteenth century. His naval career does not seem to have been a glittering one. As he told Kennedy-Cox, he was the only officer in the Great War who got a consistent 'bad report' from all his commanding officers. He seems to have suffered, as with his activities with the Church Union, from a surfeit of enthusiasm. Tom Cullen interviewed one of his superior officers, the commander of the supply ship HMS *Gibraltar*. Davidson apparently called a church parade for the crew of the *Gibraltar* each and every time a ship rendezvoused with them to collect supplies, regardless of the time of day or night. Davidson's service records are in the National Archives[3] and entirely bear out his own assessment of his abilities (or lack thereof):

> In awarding 'satisfactory' for conduct I wish to qualify the award. Mr Davidson has not actually disregarded the Naval Regulations as regards his special duties but his heart is not in the work and he performs his duties in a perfunctory manner. Not on good terms with messmates, disregards mess rules and regulations. [Service record entry for Harold Davidson, dated 29 June 1916, written by the commander of HMS *Gibraltar*.]

He was eventually transferred in October 1916 to the Red Sea aboard HMS *Fox* and, once again, scandal was not far behind. He was arrested in a police raid on a Cairo brothel. His explanation was that he was looking for a prostitute who had a severe dose of 'the clap' and was infecting his men. His explanation may well have been true but his talent for getting into monumental scrapes was already well established and sets the scene for what was to happen later. His service records contain an entry, dated 21 October 1916 and presumably written in connection with this incident, in which he is warned by his commanding officer that 'if any further unfavourable reports are received his services will be dispensed with'. In November of the same year the commander of the *Fox* rated him as 'unsatisfactory' and wrote that he was 'very unpunctual and unable to adapt himself to ship life. [He] has shown a great lack of tact and has been on bad

---

3 All service record entries are from the National Archives document ADM 6/444 (Admiralty: Service Records, Registers, Returns and Certificates, Civil Branch Officers' Service Records, vol. 6, 1905–16).

terms with a number of his messmates.' He nevertheless continued to serve aboard *Fox* for almost two years, until August 1918, when he transferred to the North Atlantic aboard HMS *Leviathan*. His commanding officer there, though hardly effusive, was a little more complimentary, writing that he was 'a clever writer and entertainer [who] pays attention to duty'.

Davidson was demobilised from the Navy on 11 March 1919 and returned to Stiffkey to resume his duties as rector. When he arrived he discovered that Molly was six months pregnant with their fifth child, Pamela. The problem was that the absent Davidson could not have been the father. His service records state that he was granted three weeks' leave in England on 24 July 1918. In other words, the latest date that he could possibly have returned to his ship was 14 August 1918. The persistent rumour at the time, perpetuated by Pamela herself in later years, was that Molly had been seduced by one of the many people who lodged at the rectory while Davidson was away serving in the war. The product of their liaison, Pamela Cushla le Poer Davidson, was born on 21 June 1919, some ten months and three days after the end of the rector's UK leave.

Davidson was fond of Pamela despite the questions over her parentage. She actually bore a strong physical resemblance to him but, right up until her death in 2001, she always claimed to be the illegitimate daughter of one of Molly's lodgers, Colonel Ernest Doudemain of the Canadian Army, Davidson's old school friend. Her obituary in the *Daily Telegraph* of 12 March 2001 is illuminating. Her life from the very beginning seems to have been full of oddities and contradictions. Davidson was an Anglican priest and yet she was educated as a Catholic at a convent school. She was only thirteen when Davidson's trial took place, and at its conclusion Molly took the children to live in Harrow. Pamela and the rector were close and she would often go to stay with him in Blackpool and Skegness. She acquired his love of the theatre and was first employed in a circus in Skegness, learning to be a trapeze artist. She subsequently made her way to London, where she worked as a chorus girl at the Windmill Theatre. A tour of Germany followed in 1938, in the course of which she was propositioned by Joseph Goebbels, Hitler's propaganda minister, and detained for a night by the Gestapo. During the war she worked for the Red Cross, entertaining American troops based in Britain, and in 1941 she married a fighter pilot, George Nelson-Edwards, DFC. After the war she produced two sons and she and her husband settled down to run a tavern in Pembrokeshire.

Davidson seems to have been utterly devastated by Molly's infidelity and their marriage never really recovered. Tom Cullen quotes an unnamed local taxi-driver (not exactly a reliable source it must be admitted), who told him that when he came to collect Davidson for the London train on Monday mornings he would see him sleeping on a couch in his study. There was also plenty of gossip in the village. The couple stayed together, probably for the sake of the children, but Davidson began to spend increasing periods of time away from home. He even applied for a one-year post as a chaplain at a hill station in India, at Simla, and hired a locum to replace him while he was away. When the post fell through, he was forced to pay the man £150 to honour the contract they had made.

In 1920 Davidson met Rosalie (Rose) Ellis, who was twenty years old, broke, and teetering on the brink of prostitution. Davidson helped her with a gift of money. One has to conclude that he acted out of chaste motives and a sense of compassion, but he was sowing the seeds of his own destruction. A streak of self-destructiveness in Harold Davidson manifested itself around the time of his first meeting with Rose Ellis. The discovery of Molly's unfaithfulness may have been at the root of it.

Whatever the reason or reasons, Davidson's choice of associates tended now to be gravely flawed. Perhaps the least felicitous choice was the Canadian bankrupt and general chancer Arthur John Gordon. Davidson appears to have been one of Gordon's first victims; he was persuaded by Gordon to invest about £5,000 in a scheme that promptly collapsed – although he does appear to have recovered at least part of the money. It was not long, however, before the activities of the pair were intertwined: the rector solicited funds from his wide circle of acquaintances to invest in Gordon's hare-brained schemes. It seems that, as a clergyman, he had little difficulty in obtaining the trust of likely investors. Two notable victims, according to Cullen's research, were Davidson's own solicitor, Harold Edwards and a fellow cleric, the Revd Hugh Boswell Chapman. Two of the more outrageous scams were an island of guano (bat droppings) which, Davidson declared, would make millions,[4] and a portfolio of untapped patents in American mines.

Davidson began to use Gordon as the excuse to keep his creditors at bay. Right up until his trial in 1932, he would repeatedly hold out the prospect of the riches with which they would all be showered when Gordon's ship finally came in. He continued his work with 'his girls'. It is clear that he felt that no woman, regardless of her circumstances or behaviour, was beyond redemption. The prevailing attitude at the time, certainly of the Church and probably of society as a whole, was to sweep the whole issue of prostitution under the carpet. Most commentators of the 1920s implied that it was engaged in by a small number of impecunious, misguided souls rather than accepting the reality – that it was widespread. In a telling incident in 1926, Davidson disrupted a performance of the play *The Outcast*. In the play Miriam, the ex-prostitute, declines to marry her lover because she feels that her past behaviour deprives her of the right to deserve happiness. At the end of a performance Davidson jumped up and began to berate the audience, telling them that Miriam 'should be treated as our sister and not as an outcast...and you, by your applause, have encouraged such attitudes'.

Davidson's troubles multiplied throughout the 1920s. He was expelled from the Royal Overseas League for pestering the telephonists. The club was founded in 1910 by Sir Evelyn Wrench to foster international understanding and friendship, but Sir Evelyn's portfolio seems not to have included the strange women who were to be seen loitering about the club's entrance and associated in members' complaints with Davidson. The rector's financial situation also deteriorated, due mainly to his dealings with Arthur Gordon, and by 1925 he was deeply in debt. In February 1925 he was in arrears with his quarterly rates and an arrest warrant was issued against him. He obtained a brief respite by borrowing money from loan sharks at an extortionate rate of interest but soon found himself unable to pay and before the courts once again. A series of court actions followed during the middle part of 1925 culminating, in October of that year, with his filing a petition for bankruptcy with declared debts of £2,924.

He was now at risk of being defrocked by the Church. Under the

4 The story of the island of guano comes from the 1970s BBC radio programme *A Proper Little Gent*. The interviewee was Ted Doudemain, son of Ernest.

Clergy Discipline Act of 1892, a clergyman could be prosecuted and tried in a Consistory Court for immoral acts or conduct. 'Immoral acts' are specified as the keeping of servile labour, drunkenness, riot, idling, gambling, adultery, swearing, ribaldry and 'other wickedness', a vague term that covers a multitude of sins. A parishioner or a bishop can bring a charge although the bishop has a right of veto. Consistory Courts are ecclesiastical courts in which a bishop administers Church law within his diocese. Established by a charter of William the Conqueror, they exist in every diocese in England. The officer who exercises jurisdiction in a Consistory Court is known as the chancellor and is appointed by a patent from the bishop or archbishop. Upon conviction the chancellor recommends the punishment – which can be a period of suspension or a complete deposition from Holy Orders – to the bishop who will then pronounce it in his cathedral. Appeals to the Judicial Committee of the Privy Council are permitted. The lords of this committee comprise five assessors appointed by the Archbishop of Canterbury, the Archbishop of York or the Bishop of London. While it is a matter for debate whether indebtedness counts as an immoral act, there is no doubt that, if Davidson's creditors had succeeded in having him sent to prison for not paying his debts, he would have been defrocked under the terms of the act. However, a settlement was eventually reached whereby he was deprived of half of his £800 annual stipend to repay his creditors. Alan Tuck, the village postman during Davidson's day, said that the rector was always strapped for cash. When he was dropped off at Wells railway station on a Monday morning to catch the London train, he would often run for the platform and leave his unfortunate taxi driver waiting for his fare.

3
Trouble Ahead

By the second half of the 1920s the pattern of Harold Davidson's life had become well established. He was to be found living in a string of rented rooms in the Russell Square, Euston and Bloomsbury areas of London, between Euston Station and the British Museum. Most of his lodgings were within reasonable walking distance of the theatres and cafés of the West End and this is where he spent his weekdays, far from his family and parish.

His financial situation, however, had not significantly improved and he had made powerful enemies in the parish. In many ways he was an entirely unsuitable choice for the post of rural rector. Ned Hamond, son of Major Philip Hamond,[1] one of the key players in the whole affair, describes Davidson as a complex character who came late to the priesthood and whose theatrical background and liberal views were bound to lead to conflict with the local Norfolk Establishment. He would have been more suited, surely, to an inner-city parish.

Ned Hamond's father came to live in Morston in 1914, moving from the Norfolk village of Twyford, near Guist, although he did not settle there properly until the war's end. He was a keen wildfowler and a frequent visitor to the Morston area long before he actually lived there. He built Scaldbeck, a large house that still stands on the edge of the marshes and is occupied by his elder son Richard, and a smaller cottage where his younger son Ned Hamond now lives. Even the most cursory of glances at Philip Hamond's background suggests a total incompatibility with someone of Davidson's liberal complexities. He had run away from school at Repton to fight with the Norfolk Regiment in the Boer War and was badly wounded. At eighteen he was the Army's youngest recipient of the DSO and by the time the First World War

1 Background detail comes from the author's interview with Ned Hamond, son of Major Hamond and his second wife Diana, on 15 February 2003, from subsequent correspondence with Ned Hamond, and from information in Tom Cullen's book.

broke out in 1914 he had reached the rank of major. He participated in the earliest tank battles, winning an MC and adding a bar to his DSO. When, with the war over, he left the Army and returned to Morston, he became a pillar of the local community: a magistrate on the Holt bench, latterly acting churchwarden in the village church and an official in the British Legion.

Hamond did not suffer fools gladly and he and Davidson began to clash almost at once. Davidson's grandson Colin St Johnston[2] says that what really made the rector unpopular with local landowners was his support for the common man. Farm labourers went through dreadful privation during the agricultural depression of the 1920s and were frequently thrown out of their jobs and summarily evicted from their cottages. Davidson was not afraid to speak up for them and was, according to St Johnston, particularly incensed by the practice among local magistrates of imposing custodial sentences for poaching. In Davidson's opinion it was perfectly understandable that a destitute man should take a pheasant or rabbit to help feed his family. But the social gulf between classes was formidable. Susan Skerry,[3] whose late father, John Jarvis, was born and raised in Stiffkey with his six brothers, gives us a painful glimpse of it. Norman Jarvis, one of the brothers, was sitting on a fence one day beside a field gate. A man on horseback approached him and Norman continued sitting on the fence and made no move to open the gate. The rider said 'Good morning, Jarvis', to which Norman replied, 'Morning.' The rider dismounted furiously, let himself through the gate and said, 'In future, when you address me, you will say *sir*!' Norman replied: 'In future, I shan't bloody speak at all!' Within days the family were turned out of their tied cottage. Skerry says that it was Davidson who saw to it that her uncle was re-housed in one of the 'courtyard' cottages near Stiffkey's bridge.

Ned Hamond describes the rector as 'a fish out of water' and says that 'from an acorn of mutual dislike' between his father and Davidson 'grew a mighty oak of hatred'. Davidson was a short dapper man who was always well turned out (as the many photographs of him will attest), but his time-keeping was terrible. He was perpetually late and was often to be seen pedalling furiously along the road to church,

2 Interview with the author, 19 April 2004.
3 Correspondence with the author, May 2005.

sometimes arriving after the congregation had grown tired of waiting and gone home. In one celebrated incident, Davidson is said to have arrived without the bread and wine for communion and was ordered, by an incandescent Major Hamond, to cycle the three or four miles back to Stiffkey to collect it.

In 1927 matters came to a head with a splenetic exchange of letters between the two men. Major Hamond's first wife Rita died in 1926 at the age of only forty, and was buried in Morston churchyard in a simple grave without a headstone. In 1927 Hamond went to the churchyard to clear away some brambles and tidy the grave. For some reason Davidson took exception to this and wrote him a letter that was breathtaking in both its rudeness and its insensitivity to a man who had been only recently bereaved:

> 4, Park Place
> St. James's
> London S.W.1
> 8th February 1927

Dear Major Hamond,

In a letter written to you about ten days ago, and twice returned by you apparently unopened and unread, I mentioned that I wished to correspond with you regarding the piece of Churchyard surrounding your wife's grave in Morston Churchyard…

I was very much surprised about a fortnight ago, when inspecting the Churchyard at Morston with a view of having the brambles, etc. cut away near the north side of the Church, to discover that without one word to me you had appropriated roughly from 280 to 288 square feet of my property, and that you had turfed it and surrounded it with a gravel border. Morston Churchyard is the private freehold property of the Rector of Morston from the day of his induction until the day of his death or resignation and you have no possible right to interfere with it in any way without my permission any more than I have to come and annex a part of your garden and carry out similar operations therein…Of course you are free to approach me to buy a piece of the Churchyard around the grave in which you are interested, and I have the right to sell it to you, or to refuse to do so…

If you are anxious to preserve to yourself the piece of ground which at the present moment you have illegally appropriated, I shall be glad to treat you with the same consideration as I treated Mrs Grey [whom Davidson permitted to purchase a plot for her husband Colonel Grey in 1920]...

Yours sincerely,
HAROLD DAVIDSON

Major Hamond's response is more or less what one would expect from a man who has just been invited, by his own parish priest, to purchase the site of his recently deceased wife's grave.

Feb. 18th 1927

Sir,

Reference your letter of 8th which was forwarded to me as I have been away from home. I gather from a somewhat profuse mass of verbiage

1) That you suppose I have appropriated any portion of Morston Church yard. This is not so.

2) That trading on the idea that I care the least where I am buried myself, you do yourself the injustice & believe that I can be 'blackmailed' (for want of a more suitable term) into buying from you Morston Church property of which you are only a tenant for life, though you possibly have the right. This is also not a fact. When I die I have no objection to being buried in or out of Morston Church yard, & I shall not care if elder bushes or brambles swamp my grave, & I daresay no one else will. It is obvious from your letter that you regard this as a Heaven sent opportunity of 'getting your own back' on me. You are wrong. If you really want to know what I have done, I have no objection to telling you. I have removed the jungle which through your own neglect & lack of interest had been allowed to grow against the Church wall where my wife's grave is, & in order to prevent any further damage to the foundations of the Church, I had it properly stubbed out & some gravel laid to prevent its reappearance... This land however is your freehold, & you had better do it yourself or neglect it as you please. I personally do not propose to do anything for or to Morston Church until it pleases Almighty God in his infinite mercy to remove you from our midst... I am not able to restore the corner where my wife lies to its original condition as

the elder trees & brambles I rooted out are now dead, & I cannot identify the broken bottles and tins that previously lay there...
I am Sir

Yours etc

PHILIP HAMOND

From this moment there existed a state of open warfare between the two men. Whatever the rights and wrongs of the antipathy that existed between them, it is undeniably true that the rector adopted a rather *laissez-faire* attitude to many of his parish duties. An examination of the burial records for Morston church for the period of Davidson's tenure, from 1906 to 1932, is extremely revealing. Throughout the entire twenty-six year period he conducted no more than handful of burials, usually deputing his curate or other vicars. There was apparently a joke among the villagers of Morston and Stiffkey that one should always endeavour to die on a Saturday or a Sunday, when Davidson was likely to be in the parish to conduct the funeral service. Wedding ceremonies, too, were usually deputed or conducted on a Sunday. Davidson's detractors said that the only time he spent a complete week in the parish was during the General Strike of 1926.

His preaching technique was in keeping with his theatrical background – he rather waffled his way through the sermon but usually came up with a dramatic flourish at the end. Dr Richard Hamond,[4] Major Hamond's elder son, recalls a conversation with Arthur Gidney, the Stiffkey village blacksmith and chairman of the parish council at the time of these events. Gidney told him that part of Davidson's appeal was his talent as a preacher. The working men and women of the village tended to be in awe of Davidson's sermons, whereas the better-educated middle classes found his manner of speaking rather circuitous. When Ted Doudemain was interviewed for *A Proper Little Gent*, he recalled that there were typically only five or six children and the churchwarden in Stiffkey church for Sunday services and that the building was full of bats. The children were each given sixpences to put in the collection plate but as soon as the service ended they all rushed round to the vestry and snatched them back.

In the same radio programme the former village postman Alan Tuck

4 Interview with the author 4 October 2003.

described a vintage piece of Davidson eccentricity. Tuck's brother manned the gatehouse on the Stiffkey Road. Davidson used to ride his bicycle past the gatehouse on his way to Wells to catch the train but was always missing it and would sometimes set the track signals to danger so that he could stop the train and clamber aboard. Tuck's brother would become so enraged by Davidson's behaviour that he would bodily pick up the 5ft 3in rector and deposit him out on the road.

In *Don't Tread on the Butterflies*, her memoir of life in Heacham and Stiffkey from 1912 to 1932, Joan Sternberg provides a colourful, child's-eye portrait of Davidson. Now dead, Mrs Sternberg appeared in *Matter of Fact*, a 1994 BBC documentary on the Davidson affair. During the programme she told the interviewer that she was so disgusted at Davidson's treatment at the hands of the ecclesiastical authorities that she never attended church again. In her memoir of village life her recollections of Davidson are vivid and precise; both his eccentricities and his undoubted charm are apparent. Sternberg lived in Heacham, her grandparents were residents of Stiffkey. She would take the train to school from Heacham every Monday morning and Davidson would board from the Wells train, on his way back to London via King's Lynn. He would seek out the girls and sit in their carriage. He was a good storyteller, spoke with the resonance and clarity of a man used to the stage and told the girls jokes that were slightly risqué by the standards of the day. The girls quite clearly adored him, and there was never the slightest suggestion of impropriety. Then on Saturday evenings Davidson, heading back to Wells from London in time for the Sunday service, would sometimes miss his connection and be forced to spend the night at Heacham. He would often sleep upright in a chair at Heacham station but would occasionally be turfed out at midnight when the stationmaster came to lock up. He would then walk to Heacham village in search of a bed, sometimes alighting at the Sternberg house. Joan's parents would give him a bed in her sister's room and the three sisters would be moved to sleep, three-in-a-bed, in another room. Davidson would often ask to peek in on the girls and leave toffees on their pillow but, as with his train journeys with the girls, there was never the faintest suggestion that his behaviour was improper.

Sternberg confirmed that Davidson was an appalling timekeeper. She frequently saw him dashing along the coast road on a bicycle or in a taxi to reach Stiffkey in time for the 11 o'clock service. On one occasion, she recalled, Davidson recruited her and her sisters as a 'rent-a-congregation' after he arrived at Stiffkey church long after the departure of his flock. He delivered the full service (including the sermon) to the girls, who had travelled with him in the taxi from Heacham to visit their grandparents. As for his young *protégées*, it had long been known that he brought them back to Stiffkey for some sea air and a break from the temptations of London life. Joan Sternberg clearly recalls seeing two or three girls at a time walking around the village. Davidson's wife would try to find them employment in one of the local houses. What stretched Major Hamond's patience to breaking point, according to Tom Cullen's account, was when the girls began to go on nocturnal expeditions from the rectory to consort with the local farm hands: 'Ordinarily the only sound to be heard in the surrounding countryside after dusk was the screech of the barn owl as it swooped on its prey, but now Stiffkey's bosky lanes echoed to the sighs and giggles of those who played at love's age-old game, and a villager out walking his dog was apt to encounter shadows that sprang apart at his approach.'

Most of his parishioners, with a few notable exceptions, believed that Harold Davidson's motives for bringing these girls to the village were unimpeachable. Susan Skerry's[5] grandmother was a staunch chapelgoer, a loyal friend to the Davidsons and a supporter of his work with young women. Her seven sons played in the rectory gardens, were given treats from the kitchen and sometimes went to supper with the rector's family and no hint of scandal ever reached her ears. Molly Davidson may have disapproved of her husband's work with 'waifs and strays' but she was a party to it and supported him too. Skerry says that her father described Davidson as a truly gentle, kindly man who felt extremely strongly that the benefits of life should be open to all. Her father told her that the only people who misinterpreted the rector's motives were the Norfolk Establishment. Philip Hamond and Mrs Grey, wife of the late Colonel Grey of Stiffkey Old Hall, were particularly vocal. Mrs Grey seems to have been an especially bitter, vindictive woman who was convinced that Davidson was up to no good with his young wards. She would, no doubt, have joined the growing clamour

5 Correspondence with the author May 2005.

to have Davidson removed from his post but she died soon afterwards in horrible circumstances. As the enmity towards Davidson intensified among a section of the village, Skerry's grandfather commented that Mrs Grey would, he believed, 'die a very slow, horrible death'. Within a matter of weeks of his remark the unfortunate lady fell into the village cesspit. Skerry's grandfather ran for help and Mrs Grey, an extremely large woman, had to be hauled out with block and tackle. She never fully recovered from the accident and died some months later.

Major Hamond's second wife Diana told Tom Cullen that her husband had spoken to a cousin who was a clergyman, and that he had suggested that a complaint be made under Article 2 of the Clergy Discipline Act of 1892. Bertram Pollock,[6] the Bishop of Norwich, is said to have been dismayed when Hamond's complaint arrived in the middle of 1931; less because of the content of the accusation than because he disliked meddling in the affairs of his clergymen. During his seventeen years as headmaster of Wellington College, Pollock was said to have been equally reluctant to dole out punishment to unruly boys. The bishop had already defended Davidson during a dinner at Holkham Hall at the beginning of 1931. Lady Leicester told Pollock the latest scandalous gossip circulating about Davidson and the bishop remarked, 'Poor Mr Davidson is much maligned.' Tom Cullen suggests, quite plausibly, that Pollock was reluctant to take sides against Davidson because he had himself been the subject of gossip and innuendo with regard to his own private life. Pollock was highly regarded during his long career as bishop but tongues had wagged when he entered into a long period of mourning over the death on 22 February 1919 of his twenty-year-old secretary, and reputed mistress, Violet Morgan (known as 'Sweet Vi'). She is buried at Caistor in Lincolnshire but there is an extravagant memorial in Norwich Cathedral – seven feet high with its plinth – of a seraphic young woman kneeling with her hands clasped in prayer. The sculptor was Derwent Wood, RA, and his creation originally stood outside the Jesus Chapel at the eastern end of the cathedral. It was moved to a corner of the north transept by Pollock's successor and is now positioned, quite deliberately, so that its rather florid inscription is invisible to visitors. One must crouch down

6 Bertram Pollock (1863–1943), KCVO, DD, Master of Wellington College 1893–1910, Bishop of Norwich 1910–42. He is buried in Norwich Cathedral.

and squint at the back of the stone to read it. To those who believe in the old adage about living in glass houses and not throwing stones, it might seem that Bishop Pollock's own accommodation was a little fragile:

In Caistor Churchyard was laid to rest by Bertram Bishop of Norwich
all that could die of Violet the lovely and beloved only child
of Penry and Evelyn Arden Vaughan Morgan
Sweet Vi who on February 22 1919 at the age of twenty years
passed from this life to the life eternal.

There is more. On the left side of the plinth is a poem reputed to have been written by Pollock himself:

No voice shall break the glory of the stillness
Or touch the joy that two souls fulfils
And we shall see the splendour
Of the morning dawn on the hills.
V.V.M.

On the right side of the plinth are some lines from *The Prelude*, Book 12, by William Wordsworth:

I knew a maid,
A young enthusiast, who escaped these bonds;
Her eye was not the mistress of her heart;
Far less did rules prescribed by passive taste,
Or barren intermeddling subtleties,
Perplex her mind; but, wise as women are
When genial circumstance hath favoured them,
She welcomed what was given, and craved no more;
Whate'er the scene presented to her view
That was the best, to that she was attuned
By her benign simplicity of life,
And through a perfect happiness of soul,
Whose variegated feelings were in this
Sisters, that they were each some new delight.
Birds in the bower, and lambs in the green field,
Could they have known her, would have loved; methought
Her very presence such a sweetness breathed,

That flowers, and trees, and even the silent hills,
And everything she looked on, should have had
An intimation how she bore herself
Towards them and to all creatures. God delights
In such a being; for, her common thoughts
Are piety, her life is gratitude.

In 1928, nine years after the death of 'Sweet Vi', there was more talk when the sixty-four-year-old Bishop Pollock married Joan Florence Helena Ryder, his housekeeper and a woman less than half his age.

We have already looked at the Clergy Discipline Act of 1892 (see page 19), under which Major Hamond now accused Davidson. It is arguable whether Major Hamond's allegation against Davidson fitted any of the specified offences and Pollock had to decide whether to veto the complaint or to initiate proceedings. In the event his legal counsel, Henry Dashwood of the firm of Lee, Bolton and Lee, advised him to investigate the accusations and to proceed if there was found to be a case. A friend of Pollock, the Revd Edward Powell, told Cullen that the bishop did not act out of vindictiveness but because he appears to have been faced by such an overwhelming body of evidence that Davidson's misbehaviour was impossible to ignore: 'In no sense was Dr Pollock a persecutor. He was a very gentle person who easily became sentimental...I am pretty sure that when Dr Pollock came to prosecute, it was clear that he had clear proofs that here was a really "criminous clerk".'[7] Of course, Powell's comments are based on hearsay and provide no solid proof of Davidson's guilt or innocence.

The London law firm of Lee, Bolton and Lee was founded in 1855 and still occupies the same premises at no. 1, The Sanctuary, Westminster. The education, charities and ecclesiastical sides of the firm's practice were strong from the very beginning and, at the time of the Davidson affair, Lee, Bolton and Lee were pre-eminent in the field of Church law. Henry (later Sir Henry) Thomas Alexander Dashwood was a senior partner with the firm, joining in 1913 and remaining for over forty years. His many important appointments included Joint Legal Secretary to the Archbishop of Canterbury, Chapter Clerk of St Paul's Cathedral, Principal Registrar of the Province of Canterbury and

7 Tom Cullen, *The Prostitutes' Padre*, *op. cit.*, page 60.

Registrar of the Court of Arches and of the Faculty Office.[8] In among
the documents in Ned Hamond's possession and examined by the
author is a letter written on 23 November 1936 by Harold Davidson
to Graham Douglas Heath, partner in Lee, Bolton and Lee and author
of the firm's 1955 centenary publication. It recalls the attempts by the
bishop's solicitors to obtain evidence against the rector during the
initial investigation in the summer of 1931. The latter paragraphs in
Davidson's letter are a masterpiece of restrained vitriol, and I reproduce
them here without comment as to their veracity:

> ... I still treasure in my memory your visits to various parishioners
> at Stiffkey, in the company of Mrs Hamond, in the early part of
> the summer of 1931, in your efforts to try and father various
> babies upon me, belonging to girls who had made foolish
> mistakes, whom my wife and I together were interested in trying
> to help. Nor have I forgotten your visit to Miss Grace, the dancing
> mistress, and the insulting suggestions you made to her.
>
> I remember, also, the night shortly before the hearing of the
> case when you were at the Windmill Café in a state of inebriation,
> endeavouring no doubt to collect evidence against me, if possible,
> when I, and some of my family, chancing to go there for supper,
> thus stumbled upon you.

Lee, Bolton and Lee hired, on the bishop's behalf, the London-based
Arrow's Detective Agency to investigate Davidson's behaviour. It was
run by Charles Arrow, an ex-Scotland Yard Chief Inspector – a competent detective but someone who was more used to inquiring into adulterous behaviour on behalf of wives or husbands seeking grounds for
divorce. He put his best detective on the case, Christopher John Searle,
and set about penetrating the somewhat feeble defences of Rose Ellis,
the woman Davidson had befriended back in 1920. During the inter-
vening years Davidson had continued to help Rose; she had even spent
a rather unsatisfactory spell living at the Stiffkey vicarage employed as
a gardener, but had soon tired of the work and moved back to London.
Davidson had also helped to find her accommodation and to obtain
treatment for a severe bout of syphilis. He had subsequently found her

8 Graham Heath, *One Hundred Years at the Sanctuary*, Lee, Bolton and Lee
company publication, 1955.

a position with a touring theatre company but drink and despondency appear to have got the better of her throughout much of the 1920s. Davidson tried various strategies to help her, including taking her to Paris to get her work as an *au pair*. It all came to nothing in the end and she was soon back in London, broke and dependent once again on the generosity of the rector. It is clear from their correspondence that the rector despaired of her:

> Dear Rosalie,
> I am enclosing you now [a] Postal Order for 2/6 not to be spent in the Half-way House, or any other place, but for fares to look for a decent job... Now that you have become a heavy alcohol soaker and are practically an habitual drunkard I cannot take any interest in you until you become a total abstainer... I am terribly sorry for you, and terribly disappointed in you.
>
> Your sincerely friend & Padre,
HAROLD F. DAVIDSON[9]

Christopher Searle, the Arrow's detective who interviewed Rose, presented her with a new coat and a total of forty shillings (two pounds) in return for two statements. The second and more important of these was taken during a meeting in the bar of the Grand Hotel in Charing Cross on 29 November 1931. Rose was accompanied by her fiancé, a young man called Billy Parsloe, and Searle proceeded to ply her with glasses of port to loosen her tongue.[10] He appears to have succeeded and a signed statement of some thirteen pages in length was extracted from her.

In the event, Rose was not called to give evidence at Davidson's trial and her statement was never introduced. However, the prosecutor did make references to Davidson's relationship with Rose, based on some of the information contained in her statement, so we do have an idea of what she said. Davidson helped her on innumerable occasions and, beyond a little secretarial work and a little sock darning, she appears to have given very little in return.

The aim of the investigators was to show that the relationship

9 Letter from Harold Davidson to Rose Ellis dated 27 October 1931. Included in the court papers at the Norfolk Record Office.
10 The number of glasses of port consumed by Rose Ellis became an issue at Davidson's trial.

between them was an improper one, but despite being paid and plied with drink the worst Rose seems to have come up with was that she had once dressed a boil on the rector's bottom. In fact, she suffered a serious attack of second thoughts the day after giving her last statement and promptly retracted it. She is reported to have told a friend, 'I made a mistake under considerable temptation, which has placed a mutual friend of ours in a terrible position, and most unjustly so.' She was to repeat this sentiment to the newspapers after Davidson's trial began, saying publicly that he was innocent.

As it was, Rose told Davidson what she had done. Given the predicament in which her statements had placed him, he showed her surprisingly little resentment; instead he seems to have become furious at the Church's underhand tactics. He wrote to Bishop Pollock on 9 December 1931, his letter a somewhat clumsy probing exercise and an attempt to ensure that Rose Ellis would not be regarded as a credible witness. Rose he describes as 'mentally defective... found to be of unsound mind... on one occasion by a court when she attempted to commit suicide'. After 'bribing her with money and drugging her with alcohol', he wrote, the inquiry agents got their statement. Davidson makes the somewhat disingenuous claim that they 'had tried to excite her jealousy by suggesting that I had grown tired of her case... and was now much more interested in the case of another much younger girl'.

Davidson appears to be in no doubt that the Bishop of Norwich had ordered or at the very least consented to the investigation. He wrote that 'the Ecclesiastical mind has been guilty in past history of using some very underhanded methods', but that he could not quite believe this latest outrage. In what was surely a further dig at the bishop he wrote: 'Evidently there must be somebody with money to waste at the back of it, but whoever it may be, I shall take the most drastic action to terminate their activities.' The investigators were guilty of 'bribery', 'corruption' and 'blackmail', he declared, and he vowed to subject them to a citizen's arrest when he caught up with them. He felt sure that he could rely on Pollock's support in 'preventing the dice being loaded' against him and told him that 'If she is called up publicly she will say that the temptation of the money made her do it, and that they made her so drunk that she did not know half the time what she was saying.'

As far as the Bishop of Norwich was concerned, the only welcome piece of news contained in the letter was Davidson's vow that he would cease waiting for Mr Gordon's ship to come in[11] and instead spend more time in his parish. The bishop's four-line response is a marvellous piece of understatement:

> Dear Mr. Davidson,
>
> Thank you for your long letter...I am glad to hear that you have now come to the conclusion that you ought long ago to have attended to my desire that you should be resident in your parish...[12]

Karilyn Collier and Colin St Johnston[13] both state that their grandfather had no idea of the precise nature of the accusations made against him until he was informed of the charges at the end of January 1932. The contents of Davidson's letter to Bishop Pollock on 9 December are open to various interpretations, but they do appear to suggest that he *did* have an idea of what was going on. It must be emphasised that at this early stage (in December 1931) there had been no decision taken by Pollock and his legal advisors either to seek Davidson's deposition from the Church or even to initiate proceedings against him. Pollock did not order charges to be laid against the rector until 8 January 1932 and even as late as 16 January, during a meeting between the two men at the Athenaeum, Davidson claimed that the bishop told him that, 'if I wished to avoid the publicity of a public trial I must resign my living unconditionally, and submit to his sentence of Deprivation. He also, himself, undertook, in these circumstances, that *I should not be Deposed from Holy Orders.*'[14] Davidson also claims that the bishop promised that he would pronounce the sentence of deprivation privately in his library, rather than subjecting the rector to the humiliation of a public spectacle in Norwich Cathedral.

11 Karilyn Collier, Davidson's granddaughter, in her account of the rector's life, suggests that Davison initially believed that the investigation concerned his dealings with Gordon and parish finances, not his activities in London. See Karilyn Collier, *Harold Francis Davidson, Rector of Stiffkey: A Biography of His Life and Trial*, Zevrika Publications, 2004.

12 Both Davidson's letter to the Bishop of Norwich dated 9 December 1931 and the latter's reply, dated 12 December 1931, are in the Norfolk Record Office.

13 Karilyn Collier (*ibid.*) and Colin St Johnston, interview with the author 19 April 2004.

14 Quoted from Harold Davidson's pamphlet, *The Reason Why*, 1934. It *is* possible for a cleric sentenced to deprivation to function as a priest with the assent of his bishop, whereas a sentence of deposition would deprive him not only of all ecclesiastical promotions but of his office as well. In other words, he would be defrocked.

Davidson held a family meeting at the Stiffkey Rectory on 10 January, attended by his wife and four of his children, during which various strategies were discussed. Molly's stance was the most obdurate of all, advising her husband: 'I should write the Bishop that you are so disgusted with the methods employed by his agents, and apparently approved by him, that you have no further use for his Spiritual Guidance... You tender your resignation and if you have any further trouble with his Lordship or his agents, you hand the whole proceedings to the Press in all its unappetising nakedness.'[15]

From Davidson's second letter to the bishop, written on 12 January, it is apparent that his attitude had hardened. This second letter was read out in full by his counsel, K. J. P. Barraclough, on 27 May 1932 at the trial and in it Davidson refers to his letter of 9 December and his initial belief that the bishop would treat the case in an even-handed manner. He makes an unequivocal declaration of his innocence although he does accept that he was not always sufficiently discreet. Perhaps heedful of Molly's advice he also indicates a willingness to consider resigning:

> You can judge therefore of my horror and distress when about three weeks later, on New Year's Eve... I realised that you yourself were ultimately responsible for the whole disgraceful business...
>
> Do you realise what a blow the duplicity of this action of yours would be to the Church which we have both loved and tried to serve according to our lights, if it became publicly known? Not one single clergyman in your Diocese could ever in future trust either your spoken or written word, the word of his Bishop and father-in-God...
>
> I can earnestly assure you in the sight of God that my conscience is free from any knowledge of a breach of the moral law either under the heading of drunkenness, or of vice in any form with women or girls, or unnatural vice with men or boys. In my particular methods of carrying on the uplifting work I have been interested in for years before I was ordained...I may not have sufficiently followed St. Paul's advice to 'avoid all appearance of

15 Statement of Molly Davidson attached to a letter written by Harold Davidson to the Bishop of Norwich on 12 January 1932. Produced as exhibit 'O' during the trial.

evil', and in my enthusiasm over certain cases I may have been indiscreet, but there is not one single young person of either sex who can in any way say they have suffered morally by my friendship...

I do realise that you may have been pushed, perhaps quite unwillingly or even unconsciously, into a terrible position by the people who acted for you as your agents...

I am ready to consider the question of resigning my living if that would help you to get out of the awkward position you have placed yourself in by having started this business in this unsavoury way...

Of course I shall be quite ready to face the public enquiry if, after our interview, you still desire it to be held, but at my wife and children's request, I shall fight it to the bitter end if forced to fight at all...

For years I have been known as the 'Prostitutes' Padre', to me the proudest title that a true priest of Christ can hold. I believe with all my soul that if He were born again in London in the present day He would be found constantly walking in Piccadilly.[16]

At the meeting with Pollock at the Athenaeum on 16 January, Davidson did indeed offer to resign but on condition that all charges against him be withdrawn. He would then submit to a private investigation and, if no evidence were found, he should be fully exonerated and restored to his post. Pollock took advice from Henry Dashwood and it was quickly decided that the proposal was not viable. Dashwood had, in fact, held several face-to-face meetings with the rector between 31 December 1931 and 21 January 1932. Davidson describes the tone of Dashwood's approach in his pamphlet *The Reason Why*. Dashwood repeatedly urged him to quit, and at each meeting presented him with a resignation letter to sign. According to Davidson, Dashwood reiterated the Bishop of Norwich's promise that the sentence of deprivation would be a low-key affair; it would be pronounced in Norwich Cathedral at an early hour when there was no one about. Dashwood's notes on their first meeting reveal a rather contemptuous attitude towards the rector:

16 Preserved in the Norfolk Record Office. The letter was also quoted widely in the press – for example in the *Eastern Daily Press* of 28 May 1932.

He could not stop talking throughout the hour and a half he was with me... Mr Davidson brought with him a deep dispatch box...disclosing a mass of letters, many in envelopes, and some bundles of envelopes. He also seemed to have inexhaustible pockets full of correspondence, etc., and I was struck by the readiness with which he found easily among this debris the letter or photograph suitable to prove the point for the time being he was making.[17]

The prosecuting counsel at the trial would make much of the fact that Davidson had confided the secret of Pamela's parentage to Dashwood during one of their meetings, on 1 January 1932. He had told Dashwood in strict confidence and the bishop's man had vowed that the information would not be introduced in evidence. During the trial the prosecution broke its word in spectacular fashion.

On 20 January Davidson's sister Muriel Alice Cox wrote a letter of supplication to his old friend Dr Arthur Winnington-Ingram, Bishop of London.[18] She writes that no one, not even Davidson, is aware that she has written, and implores the bishop to use his influence to secure a private hearing for her brother to spare the family the shame of a public trial. The Bishop of Norwich had, she said, given Davidson until 1 pm on the following day to resign his living and submit to a sentence of deprivation. The family would never agree to this, Muriel wrote, without knowing the exact nature of the charges because it would amount to an admission of guilt. The alternative, a public trial, would destroy the family's name and also, in her view, damage the reputation of the Church. She concedes that some of her brother's actions may have been 'unwise' and vows that in future that he will 'be more discreet' but implores the bishop to intervene.

In his pamphlet *The Reason Why* Harold Davidson claims that when it became apparent to the Bishop of Norwich that he intended to fight the case to the bitter end, Pollock's nerve began to falter. Pollock rushed to London on 1 February 1932, intending to withdraw the immorality charges laid under the Clergy Discipline Act of 1892 and replace them

17 Memo written by Henry Dashwood of his 1 January 1932 meeting with Harold Davidson. Cited in Cullen, *ibid.*, page 69.
18 Letter from Mrs Muriel Cox to the Bishop of London, 20 January 1932. A draft survives among the papers of the rector's grandson Colin St Johnston.

with less serious charges under the 1926 Clergy Discipline Ordinance. Unfortunately for all concerned he took the decision too late. He arrived in the capital just as the early editions of the *London Evening News* were hitting the stands. The 1 February edition gave details of the charges that had been laid against Davidson and included his categorical denial. The cat was now well and truly out of the bag – by the following day the national papers had the story and a feeding frenzy commenced. The *Daily Express* of 2 February, for example, had the story on its front page under the following headline:

RECTOR TO
FACE
CHARGES
BISHOP CALLS A
SPECIAL
COURT

RESCUE WORK
ACCOUNT
"I AM NOT GUILTY"

It is no exaggeration to compare the level of media interest in this case to that witnessed during the Profumo Scandal of the 1960s or, more recently, during the Bill Clinton-Monica Lewinsky episode in the United States. The public's fascination with the case grew more and more intense as the case unfolded. The following are a selection of headlines drawn from 1932 editions of the main Norfolk paper, the *Eastern Daily Press,* from just before and during the trial. None of the stories succeeded in bouncing the Davidson affair off the front pages:

Japanese Army on Chinese Border (8 January)

Attempt to Assassinate Japanese Emperor (9 January)

Mutiny in Dartmoor Prison (25 January)

Furious Fighting at Shanghai (30 January)

Nearly 254 M.P.H. – Malcolm Campbell's New World Record
(25 February)

Lindbergh Baby Kidnapped (3 March)

Davidson began a campaign to defend himself in the newspapers, creating an immediate sensation. His theatrical background put him in good stead and he rampaged around the country accusing the Church of hypocrisy and portraying himself as another Archdeacon Wakeford.[19] He gave an interview to the *Daily Mirror* on 2 February in which he claimed that his enemies had misrepresented his attempts to help desperate and impoverished girls. He took some of the girls to Stiffkey, he said, 'where my wife and I have looked after them until the time came for them to have their babies'. Even this had been misconstrued: it was 'a Christian thing to do... but perhaps some people thought I was the father of all those children.'

Davidson's first full account of the events leading up to the charges against him appeared in the *Empire News* on 7 February, with the publication allegedly paying him £750 for the privilege of an exclusive. Rose Ellis also went to the papers; her story appeared on 4 February on the front page of the *Daily Herald*. She accused the bishop's investigators of bribing her to make incriminating statements about the rector. The Bishop of Norwich took out a restraining order against both publications and on 22 February they were each fined for contempt of court and forbidden to comment further on the case until its conclusion.

Several of Davidson's friends rushed to defend him in the press. Among them was an actress called Mae Douglas whom Davidson had helped to embark on a stage career some twenty years before. In an interview with the *Daily Herald* on 5 February she stated that he was one of her best friends; that she trusted him implicitly and had, she said, left her fifteen-year-old daughter in his care on many occasions while she performed on stage. The girl's name was Estelle Douglas and she, and her own stage aspirations, were to play a decisive role in the events that were to follow.

Any lingering hopes among the bishop's party that Davidson would go quietly were utterly dispelled on Sunday 7 February. Davidson delivered his usual Sunday sermon in Stiffkey church, his first since the story

---

19 Archdeacon John Wakeford (1859–1930) was accused of adultery with an unidentified woman at the Bull Hotel, Peterborough, in April 1920. He was tried before a Consistory Court in Lincoln in February 1921, found guilty and defrocked. He eventually went mad trying to clear his name and died in February 1930 in a lunatic asylum.

broke. Newspaper accounts of the day's events reveal Davidson as a consummate actor:

> Motoring from London during Saturday night, the Rev. Harold Francis Davidson, rector of Stiffkey, Norfolk, after breakfasting at Sheringham, arrived at the village of Stiffkey at 10.49 yesterday morning. Quickly putting on his clerical robes, and wearing three war medals, he walked at a brisk pace straight to the Church of St. Mary. A report had been noised abroad that the rector was going to make a statement from the pulpit of a personal character. The congregation all told numbered about sixty. In the course of his sermon the Rector said that Jesus Christ... passed through every possible experience of human life that we can ever pass through from the cradle to the grave.... Throughout His public ministry He was completely misunderstood. All His actions were attributed to a spirit of evil which had got hold of Him. They called Him a drunkard, and a consort of publicans and sinners, forgetting that what He had come into the world to do was to save these people...[20]

There is no doubt to whom Davidson is referring here – the story is littered with references to Christ and to how his sufferings may be compared to those of the rector. He also told his congregation that the publicity surrounding the case was not something that he relished, despite the fact that his story, sold to the *Empire News*, was appearing that day: ' I wish to explain that ... people tell me it is possibly bad taste – all this publicity. To me personally it is exceedingly distasteful.'[21]

Evensong that Sunday was even more dramatic. The papers reported that buses brought people from neighbouring towns and villages and a congregation of 500 thronged the church. Davidson told a reporter that he would vigorously contest the charges laid against him and the crowd cheered as he left the church at the conclusion of the service. Public opinion was swinging Davidson's way, at least among the working classes, but on 9 February the hatches opened and the first of a series of bombshells was dropped. On that day, seventeen-year-old Barbara Gwendoline Harris sat down and wrote a letter to the Bishop of

20 *Eastern Daily Press* article, 8 February 1932.
21 *Eastern Daily Press, ibid.*

Norwich. A copy survives in the Norfolk Record Office with key sections underlined by the trial judge with a red pencil. The effect of the letter, when it was introduced in evidence at the trial, was seismic:

16, Providence Place
Shepherd's Bush

Dear Sir,

I am writing about the Rev. H. F. Davidson. I have been waiting to do this for a long time and mentioned it to the Rev. Davidson, and he told me I would not be believed, or my word would not stand against his. I am thinking that if he is let off he will do just the same and I am sorry for the girls in future. You will have noticed that Davidson only helps girls, never boys, and also the girls are generally about 16 or 17 years old. I am 17 years old and he has known me for 18 months. Davidson pretends he knew nothing about the charges made against him until a few days ago but he often used to say I should keep my voice low when talking to him, as detectives were following, and sometimes only one man was behind. A lot of people will stick up for Davidson because they are afraid of their past, others might stand up for him because they believe him to be an accentric [*sic*] nice old man (as I did when I first met him).

I know lots of things against him that may help you.

I think my word can be believed.

All this in Sincerity.

BARBARA HARRIS

I know. He has the keys of a lot of girls flats and front doors.[22]

The wheels of justice began to turn more quickly through February and March of 1932. There was a hearing on 17 February before Mr F. Keppel North, Chancellor of the Norwich Consistory Court. The hearing attracted little more than a paragraph in the newspapers but was actually critical to the final outcome of the case. Davidson's counsel applied for a postponement to allow more time to prepare his defence

22 Extracts from letter from Barbara Harris to Bishop Pollock, 9 February 1932. Its detailed contents are dealt with during the account of the trial. The letter contains a number of anomalies that are discussed in detail on pages 156–8.

and Humphrey King, counsel for the bishop, requested that the proceedings be heard in London rather than in Norwich. The latter request would make it easier and less costly for the large number of London-based witnesses and journalists to attend.

Both applications were accepted, on the condition that the defence *did not apply to have the case heard by assessors rather than judged solely by North*. The defence agreed and in so doing probably committed a major tactical blunder before the trial had even begun. The issue was whether or not Chancellor North would be impartial: he was a personal friend of Bishop Pollock, was godfather to his daughter, and would have been aware from the start that an acquittal would cause serious damage to the Church's reputation. In contrast, if the trial occurred within Davidson's diocese and with assessors rather than with a single judge, he would be more certain to receive a sympathetic ear. In the event the trial date was set for 29 March in the Great Hall of Church House, Westminster,[23] with North presiding.

23 The original Church House, the venue for Harold Davidson's trial, was commissioned in 1902 to commemorate the 1887 Golden Jubilee of Queen Victoria. In 1931 it was decided that the existing building would be demolished and a new structure, more suited to the current needs of the Church, would be erected. Because of the parlous state of the global economy at that time, building work was delayed until 1937 and the new Church House, designed by the renowned architect Sir Herbert Baker, was finally completed in June 1940. In November of the same year it withstood a direct hit from a German bomb with surprising resilience – a tribute to the soundness of its construction. During the war the government requisitioned the building for use by both Houses of Parliament and some of the great historic speeches and events of the era took place within its walls.

4

The Trial Begins

There was a brief, slightly comic prelude to the dramatic events of March 1932. On 7 March the rector was the subject of a summons brought before magistrates in the North Norfolk town of Walsingham.[1] He was accused of riding his bicycle in Stiffkey without a light. Davidson, not surprisingly given the pressures building in London, could not attend and wrote to the court to request an adjournment. By the time the case came up again a month later he was facing rather more serious charges.

Harold Davidson's trial opened at 10 am on Tuesday 29 March before the Norwich Consistory Court at Church House, Westminster. First to arrive was Barbara Harris, the prosecution's star witness, who posed for the ranks of press photographers[2] on the steps of the court. Newspaper photographs of Barbara show her dressed to the nines and smiling broadly; she was attired entirely in black except for an emerald green straw hat and she was clearly enjoying herself enormously. Davidson, dressed in clerical grey, arrived shortly afterwards with his wife. He was greeted by a group of supporters, including some of his parishioners from Stiffkey, and strode into the court smoking his characteristic cigar and carrying his papers in a cheap, cardboard attaché case. The proceedings were of immediate public interest and the gallery seats were filled with journalists, curious onlookers and a contingent of down-and-outs from the homeless hostel around the corner. A reporter for the *Star* noted a solitary female seated among the fifty or sixty men in the public gallery; a tall, mysterious figure dressed in a vivid scarlet costume and a black hat.[3] Davidson took his seat immediately behind his defence counsel and proceedings began.

1 *Eastern Daily Press* article 8 March 1932.
2 As A. J. P. Taylor points out in *English History, 1914–1945*, proceedings in Consistory Courts were not covered by a ban, imposed in 1926, on the publication of proceedings in divorce courts. Consistory Courts became, in Taylor's words, 'the richest source for the popular Sunday newspapers'.
3 For some clues as to the possible identity of this woman please see pages 163–4.

The Bishop of Norwich brought five charges against Davidson under the 1892 Clergy Discipline Act. They were:

1 The defendant had been guilty of immoral conduct from September, 1921, until November, 1931, with a woman named.[4]

2 The defendant, in or about the month of August 1929, was guilty of immoral conduct in that he annoyed and made improper suggestions to a waitress at a café in Walbrook, London.

3 The defendant was, on 12th November 1931, guilty of an immoral act, in that he embraced a young woman[5] in a public room at a Chinese restaurant at Bloomsbury.

4 The defendant had during the last five years been guilty of an immoral habit, in that he had habitually associated himself with women of a loose character for immoral purposes.

5 He had been guilty of the immoral habit of accosting, molesting, and importuning young females for immoral purposes.

The fifth charge had been added the day before and to this charge, as to all of the others, the rector responded with an emphatic 'Not guilty'. Chancellor North prepared to hear the case, presented by two formidable legal teams: the counsel for the bishop consisted of Roland Oliver KC, Walter Monckton KC and Humphrey King;[6] while Davidson's counsel were Richard Levy, Ryder Richardson and K. J. P. Barraclough.

Proceedings began with Chancellor North producing an anonymous letter that he had received that morning. It was passed to counsel to read and then returned without the contents being disclosed. Tom Cullen describes it in his book as a 'crank letter', one of many received during the trial, and it was quickly decided that it had no material bearing on the case. (It was signed 'GOD', which hardly reinforced its authenticity.) Roland Oliver then stood up to open the case for the

---

4 sc. Rose Ellis.
5 sc. Barbara Harris.
6 Roland (later Sir Roland) Oliver acted as junior prosecuting counsel in the notorious Thompson-Bywaters murder trial of 1922. Edith Thompson and her P&O steward lover, Frederick Bywaters, were convicted at the Old Bailey of murdering Edith's husband Percy, a shipping clerk. Both were hanged in January 1923. Roland Oliver went on to become a High Court judge. He was assisted at the Davidson trial by Walter Monckton (1891–1965). Monckton's career flourished after the Davidson affair. He served as legal advisor to King Edward VIII (drafting his 1936 abdication speech), and was Minister of Labour in Churchill's 1951 government. He was created Viscount Monckton of Brenchley in 1957.

prosecution. His address lasted for over two hours and the main thrust (if the pun might be forgiven) was that Harold Davidson had, for years, been systematically misbehaving himself with young women. He described the rector's weekly routine – Sundays in the parish and the rest of the week in London – and said that his weekday life was characterised by two obsessions. The first of these was the eternal pursuit of the elusive Mr Gordon and the promise of the £5,000 that was owed to him. The second was his fondness for associating with young women of the age of sixteen and upward. He took his girls to the theatre or cinema, paid for restaurant meals and taxis, and paid for their lodgings. The question Oliver wanted to ask was 'How did he pay for it all?' Oliver told the court that the rector had been an undischarged bankrupt since 1925 with a wife and five children to support. He also found it strange that the subjects of Davidson's charitable work were always young, attractive women and never, for example, young men.[7] The bishop's investigators also discovered, Oliver said, that the times and places at which Davidson met these women was highly significant. He met them in bedsitting rooms at all hours of the day and night; a curious place, said Oliver, to proselytise to young women.

Oliver dealt first with the fourth charge, that Davidson had 'during the last five years been guilty of an immoral habit, in that he has habitually associated himself with women of a loose character for immoral purposes'. This charge related to Barbara Harris, to a young blonde actress with the colourful name of Mrs Betty Beach, and many others who were not named by the court. When Davidson first met Barbara in September 1930, the court was told, she was only sixteen and a half years old. She was living in a ten-shillings-a-week bedsit in the rear of a tenement in Alderney Street, Victoria, and was out of work and broke. She and Davidson first met at Marble Arch. The rector approached her – not wearing clerical dress – and uttered his usual line, telling her that she looked like Mary Brian the American movie actress, and they went off to a restaurant together. The court would hear that it was months before Barbara discovered that he was a clergyman; she eventually saw some letters in his lodgings that revealed the truth. She told him of her circumstances and Davidson immediately offered to help her

7 This description of Davidson's activities in London is not entirely accurate. His early work in London, as we have seen, was with young East End boys.

to find work. He called at her lodgings the next day and her landlady would tell the court that that he described himself as her uncle. During their eighteen-month association, while she lived in the Alderney Street bedsit, Davidson would arrive at all times of the day and often gave her small amounts of money including, on occasion, paying her rent. The court would hear that he made numerous attempts to seduce her, all rebuffed. His 'technique' was alleged to involve kissing her, putting his arms around her and (somewhat bizarrely) sitting on *her* knee.

Oliver told the court that Davidson frequently took her to his London lodgings, in Macfarlane Road, Shepherd's Bush. On one occasion Barbara missed her last Tube home to Victoria and slept the night in Davidson's bed, although even the prosecution conceded that the rector slept in a chair. On 21 November 1930 Barbara was turned out of her own lodgings and went to live with a boyfriend, a married Indian high-ranking police officer in town for the Round Table Conference.[8] Davidson was on cordial terms with both of them and, the court was told, on occasion the couple sat in bed together in their pyjamas and served the rector tea. The court would hear that Barbara had light-heartedly asked him what he thought of her pyjamas, to which he is said to have replied he 'would rather have me without them'.

The Indian returned to his home country in January 1931 and Barbara, at Davidson's suggestion, moved into a back room of the house in Macfarlane Road. Barbara would testify to the court that Davidson would knock on her door at all hours of the day or night and would make indecent suggestions to her. She would tell the court that she always repelled his advances but continued, out of desperation, to accept his financial help. On occasion he would tap on her door or bathroom window in the middle of the night until she let him in. For several months, Oliver said, they actually lived together in the same room. At first the rector slept in a chair, then on the bed and, finally, in the bed with Barbara. He would also appear in front of her with no clothes on.

Rose Ellis, according to the prosecution's case, was a frequent visitor to the Macfarlane Road house and Davidson would kiss and hug each girl in front of the other. In July 1931 Davidson had the idea to send the

8 The First Round Table Conference was held in London at St James's Palace on 12 November 1930, to consider the future of India.

two girls to stay at the vicarage in Stiffkey. He was by this time already under surveillance by the bishop's investigators and was observed taking the girls shopping and to lunch before depositing them on the 3 o'clock train to Wells-next-the Sea, the closest station to Stiffkey. When they arrived at the rectory Davidson's wife set them to work, one as a maid and one as a cook, with no wages and no communication from the absent rector as to when they could leave. After a month of servitude the girls gave up waiting for Davidson to send them the fare back to London and fled. They walked to Wells and slept for two nights in fields near the station, waiting for Davidson to return and pay for their tickets home. They eventually gave up waiting and walked to Fakenham (about ten miles from Wells), where they were able to persuade a couple with a car to give them a lift back to London.

Oliver would call Barbara's sister, Sylvia Harris, to the stand. Sylvia was a lady's maid, and would tell the court that she, Barbara, Davidson, and her boyfriend had all met on one occasion at the Macfarlane Road house. On that occasion Davidson had pointed to the bed and told Sylvia that Barbara had slept in it for two or three months while he had slept in the chair. On another occasion, Sylvia would tell the court, she was at Euston Square visiting Barbara when Davidson telephoned. She listened in on the conversation and overheard the rector address her sister as 'Darling' and 'Queen of My Heart'. Barbara asked him, 'What about the other? What about Betty [i.e. Betty Beach]?', to which Sylvia heard him reply, 'Darling, I have given them all up.'

Oliver then elaborated on Betty Beach's role in the case. He told the court that on 30 October 1931 the rector took Barbara to Betty Beach's flat in Marylebone. In fact, the court would hear, Davidson had a key to Mrs Beach's flat and came and went as he pleased. Mrs Beach was at home in her nightgown and after the rector had kissed and embraced her, she is said to have put on a gymnastic display for her guests. She then dressed and Davidson took the two women to a dance school where he paid for dancing lessons.

The prosecution stated that Sylvia Harris disliked the rector and disapproved of his friendship with Barbara. The prosecution would present evidence that this friendship was inappropriate – a waitress at a Chinese restaurant in Bloomsbury would say that on 12 November 1931 she had seen Davidson kissing and fondling Barbara. The bishop's agents had seen them together on 8 October – Barbara was seen trying to shake off the rector at an Underground station (she would later give evidence that she had given him a black eye). Further, the court would hear that on 22 November Barbara rented a room for a week in order, it would be suggested, to escape from his clutches. On the same day he wrote her a letter, which would be produced in court, in which he ticked her off for her rudeness to him and demanded that she meet him later at the same Chinese restaurant.

In December Davidson installed Barbara in a bedsit owned by a Mrs Alice Lake in Providence Place, Shepherd's Bush, and found her a job. Mrs Lake would tell the court that the bedsit was previously occupied by a Lyons teashop waitress called Miss Pritchard; also a friend of Davidson. He would call at all times of the day or night and Barbara would often refuse to see him or Mrs Lake would forbid him to enter.

After Davidson realised that he was under investigation by the bishop's agents, he had gone to see Mrs Lake to ask her if anyone had been making inquiries about him. He also appears to have made deliberate efforts to undermine Barbara's credibility by telling Mrs Lake that Barbara had been in prison. This was proof, in the eyes of the prosecution, that Davidson knew Barbara's evidence would lead to his conviction. Oliver then raised the issue of the parentage of Davidson's fifth child – a subject that Henry Dashwood had promised would never be mentioned in court. Oliver told the court that the rector had said to Barbara on more than one occasion that Pamela was not his child and that he would divorce his wife and marry her.

The second charge was dealt with next, the allegation that Davidson had annoyed and made improper suggestions to a waitress at a café in Walbrook, London. The charge was significant because the girl involved was perfectly respectable, was in employment, and did not need 'rescuing'. The girl concerned was a Miss Dorothy Burn, a Lyons teashop waitress or 'nippy', as they were popularly known. Davidson developed a fixation on the girl and would sometimes visit her twice a day, would take hold of her hand and would follow her around as she worked. Davidson 'pestered this unfortunate girl to death', said Oliver, inviting her out for dates, telling her that she was too pretty to be a waitress and waving bundles of pound notes in front of her. He also told her, the prosecution alleged, 'When you get married I will perform the ceremony, and you will have eight children.'

The fifth charge – 'accosting, molesting, and importuning young females' –was really a continuation of the second. The point, Oliver said, was that these particular women did not need rescuing and were not people with whom a middle-class country cleric would be ordinarily expected to socialise. Three waitresses at the ABC café in Oxford Street were singled out in particular. Davidson had pestered them all mercilessly, inviting them out on dates, 'pawing' them, admiring their hair and, bizarrely, their teeth. Eventually there were complaints and Davidson was barred from the restaurant. Oliver went on to refer to a girl called Nellie Churchill, for whom Davidson had rented a room in October 1929 in Wharton Road, Bloomsbury. Davidson told the landlady that he employed Nellie as an artist's model three days a week and paid frequent visits to her, despite owing some £3 in rent. On one occasion, the court would hear, the landlady discovered them alone together in the dark late at night.

Oliver then addressed the first charge, that the defendant had been guilty of immoral conduct from September 1921 until November 1931 with Rose Ellis. Rose was referred to as a woman of thirty who had been of 'immoral character' for a number of years and who had known Davidson for ten. Oliver did not propose to call her as a witness for the reason that it would be pointless to place any reliance on her word (in fact she had recanted the statements she had made to the bishop's agents). Instead of calling her he asked the court to assume that the first charge, with which her name was linked, was true. Davidson had, Oliver said, referred to Rose as slow-witted and had described her at various times as his secretary and his ward. This had not, however, prevented the rector from visiting her rooms in Euston Street at all hours and from taking her to Paris.

Oliver concluded his opening address by reading extracts from Davidson's articles in the press, written just as the case broke as part of a pre-emptive attempt to garner public support. In February the *Empire News* and *Daily Herald* (which printed Rose's rebuttal) had both been fined for contempt of court and were forbidden to comment further on the case until its conclusion. Oliver asked, 'Would any educated Christian man think this a decent thing to do when he was waiting for his trial, and the case was *sub judice*?'

Oliver called his first witness, the person on whom the entire case hinged: Barbara Gwendoline Harris. She took the stand, resplendent in her emerald green hat, and told the court that she was born on 4 May

1914, had not seen her mother for three years and had never seen her father. During her examination by Oliver she confirmed, sometimes embellished, and occasionally contradicted the basic facts of the case provided by the prosecutor during his introductory address. The court heard about her first meeting with Davidson at Marble Arch. She was questioned about 'Uncle Harold' (as he described himself to her landlady) and his visits to her bedsit:

Oliver: How did he behave?
Barbara: He was quite all right most of the time.
Oliver: When he did not behave quite all right what did he do?
Barbara: He always apologised.
Oliver: What did he do?
Barbara: He started kissing me and caressing me.

Barbara told the court that almost every day Davidson gave her small amounts of money. When he came to see her one morning she was in bed in her pyjamas and he tried to kiss her. When she pushed him off he apologised. He was always kissing her, she said, and had asked her 'to give myself body and soul to him just once'.

Oliver: I am sorry to trouble you, but we must have this in evidence. What did he do?
Barbara: He tried to have intercourse with me.
Oliver: You would not?
Barbara: No.

She stayed the night on two occasions in Davidson's room in Shepherd's Bush; the rector had slept on a chair and she stated unequivocally that they did not have intercourse. Barbara affirmed what Oliver had said during his introductory address, that the pair had ended up in bed together at the Macfarlane Road house, but she had resisted his attempts to seduce her. In her evidence she claimed that, when she repulsed the rector's advances, he had on two or three occasions 'relieved himself'. This was, of course, not recorded in any of the newspaper reports about the case but is in the court papers. She told the court that the rector had first climbed into bed wearing the top half of his pyjamas and described in detail an appendectomy scar on the right hand side of his stomach. She repeated a joke that Davidson had told her about a Scotsman sitting with his girlfriend in Hyde Park. He asks her if she would like to see where his appendix was removed. The girl tells him, 'Not here', at which point the Scotsman leads her across the park, points to St George's Hospital and says, 'That is the place.' Chancellor North was deeply unamused by this attempt at levity and remarked, 'I have never heard a joke with less joke in it.' Barbara also stated that Davidson kept a box of what she referred to as 'preventatives' in a trunk by the door of his room at Macfarlane Road, although this too was neatly excised from all of the press reports.

Oliver questioned her about her criminal record – she had been remanded in Holloway Prison for a week for stealing hospital clothes (from the clinic where she was being treated for venereal disease). She claimed that it had all been a misunderstanding and she was eventually released without charge. She had also been arrested and fined for the offence of 'obstructing the footway' – a polite euphemism for streetwalking – although her version of events was that the 'obstruction' was her dog, tripped over by someone while they were out walking in the park. Both arrests occurred before she met Harold Davidson. There appears little doubt that Barbara had, on occasion, resorted to prostitution to support herself but she did so in an 'amateur' and infrequent fashion. She was treated for V.D. but denied emphatically that she actually had it. Tom Cullen suggests, quite plausibly, that she may have turned on Davidson because she resented his attempts to dissuade her from becoming a career prostitute.

Barbara was then questioned about the rector's promise to divorce his wife and marry her:

> Oliver: Did he ever tell you about his wife?
> Barbara: Yes. He said that he very seldom saw her, only once a week, and that she did not like him, that he did not like her, and that she got jealous because he had so many girls. He said that he would get a decree because the last child was not his. He would then marry me.

At this point Oliver interjected that he had seen Davidson smile and laugh aloud at this part of Barbara's evidence. Davidson denied that he had laughed but North declared, 'I did not see him, but if he did it is a very wrong and disgraceful thing to laugh at things of this sort and I will not allow it.'

The details of Barbara's explanation for Davidson's absence from the

Armistice Day celebration of 11 November 1931 were a little less salacious but no less damning. She alleged that Davidson had intended to
catch a 5 am train, to reach Stiffkey in time to lead the 11 am service,
but had missed it. He sent a telegram to his parish, explaining that he
would not be there but would go to the Cenotaph instead. Oliver
pressed her for detail about the incident and her terse responses, at a
time when the trauma of the Great War was still a highly emotive issue,
were like knife thrusts to Davidson's reputation:

> Oliver: Why did he miss the train?
> Barbara: He was trying to kiss me all the time.
> Oliver: Did he go to the Cenotaph?
> Barbara: No.

While she was living at Macfarlane Road, Barbara testified, Davidson had brought home a young woman called Miss Taylor at two in the
morning. He had taken Miss Taylor into an adjoining bedroom, saying
that he wished to show her some photographs, and then remained in
there for an hour with the lights off. Barbara claimed that there was
very little of a religious nature in her own relationship with the rector.
He had suggested to her that she pray and told her, 'God did not mind
sins of the body, only sins of the soul, and any sins of the body would be
forgiven.'

Oliver read out several letters written by Davidson to Barbara. She
had alleged that the rector had said to her, 'I do not like you; I love you',
but the letters presented at the trial and now preserved in the Norfolk
Record Office tell a different story. They are consistently matter of fact
and businesslike, and there is nothing in any of them to suggest that the
pair were lovers. In the letters presented in court Davidson alternately
praises or admonishes Barbara's behaviour, and his usual sign-off is
paternalistic, not prurient – he calls himself 'Your sincere friend and
Padre'. Most concern his attempts to find her gainful employment or
accommodation but there are references to more turbulent incidents as
well.

In one letter Davidson refers to her having insulted him at a Tube
station. The prosecution probed the incident and Barbara said that
Davidson had approached her while she was with someone else and
handed her 3s.6d, telling her that being a guardian was a great responsibility. She had knocked the money from his hand (the implication

being that he believed her to have been with a paying customer). A final humiliation on this first day of the trial was Barbara's revelation that Davidson was broke, owed money everywhere and was waiting desperately for the elusive Mr Gordon to come to his rescue.

On the second day of the trial, Wednesday 30 March, Barbara – in her green hat and fox stole – beamed for the press photographers once again. Davidson, late as usual, bustled into the court twenty minutes after proceedings began. Barbara faced cross-examination from Davidson's counsel Richard Levy. In a quiet voice Levy immediately began to focus on her promiscuity in an attempt to destroy her credibility:

> Levy: For your age you have had a very considerable experience of men?
> Barbara: Yes.
> Levy: I do not want to put it insultingly, but merely so that one can get the atmosphere of it. You have had intercourse with many men?
> Barbara: Yes.
> Levy: White men?
> Barbara: Yes.
> Levy: Black men?
> Barbara: Indians.
> Levy: Men of other kinds?
> Barbara: No.

Levy asked her about her attendance at St George's Hospital[9] in September 1930, to be treated for venereal disease. She conceded that she had attended the hospital but claimed that she had only *thought* she had the disease. Levy seized on this and questioned how Davidson could have been so foolhardy as to pursue her sexually over a period of more than a year when he believed her to be suffering from an infectious disease. She agreed that it was foolish for him to have done it but did not retract what she had said. Levy pointed out that Davidson had actually tried to divert her from the path her life was following, to find her employment, and to show her 'a little of family life and affection in

9 St George's Hospital, founded in 1733, is one of London's oldest hospitals. Now in Tooting, for over 250 years it was at Hyde Park Corner in the building now occupied by the Lanesborough Hotel.

order to change [her] mode of life'. He questioned her account of their first meeting at Marble Arch – rather than trying to pick her up with his line about her resemblance to Mary Brian the movie actress, he had, Levy suggested, warned her that the woman she was talking to at the time was a procuress:

Levy: Do you know what that means?
Barbara: I suppose it means the white slave traffic.
Levy: Did you say you were out of work?
Barbara: He thought I was a typist because I had an attaché case in my hand. That was after he said he thought I was a film star.
Levy: You have always fancied yourself as a prospective film star?
Barbara: Never. I should hate to work for the films.
Levy: Why?
Barbara: I cannot face the cameras.
Levy: You seem to have done so very successfully outside here yesterday, judging by...this morning's newspapers. (Laughter.)

Levy also disputed her assertion that Davidson had tried to seduce her on numerous occasions in the Alderney Street bedsit when, as he pointed out, the door to her room had no lock:

Levy: There was a lock that would not work, is that right?
Barbara: Just an ordinary knob on it... a handle.
Levy: There was no key to fit it?
Barbara: No.
Levy: So if he were endeavouring, as you say, to force his attentions upon you, he always had to do it with an open door in the sense that it had no lock, and your landlady or anybody else could walk in at any moment?
Barbara: Yes.

Levy went on to dispute Barbara's claim that Davidson had pushed her back onto the bed, suggesting that it was she who had made advances to the rector:

Levy: Is not this what happened, that when he came into the room you suddenly went up to him and kissed him on the lips and forced your tongue into his mouth?
Barbara: No.

Levy: And then he pushed you back onto the bed when you did that?

Barbara: I did not do that.

Levy: And did you throw your legs round him, and did he say, 'What are you doing?' And did you say, 'Making love with my legs'?

Barbara: I never said anything of the sort and never did anything of the sort.

The seventeen-year-old Barbara Harris was, without doubt, a woman of some considerable sexual experience: she admitted in court to having had around a dozen lovers during the previous two years. Levy made concerted efforts to paint her as a 'scarlet woman', preying on the upright, pure-hearted Harold Davidson. The problem for Levy was that Barbara was a formidable witness. Her responses throughout the trial were precise, unemotional and often damning. Davidson himself conceded this; Tom Cullen quotes him as saying that 'she was the best witness under a trying ordeal I have ever seen'. Levy tried another tack, attempting to portray her as workshy. Why, he asked, if Davidson was so repulsive to her, did she keep going back to him for help? Her reply was that she wanted him to get her a job and also to provide her with a reference. Chancellor North seemed unimpressed:

North: It has dawned on me long ago that this girl is the sort that, if she can get anything out of anybody, she does.

The court heard that Barbara worked for a brief spell as a domestic in Villiers Street, Charing Cross, but it did not last and from her comments throughout the trial it is clear that she was singularly uninterested in the notion of working as a maid. Her next stop after Villiers Street was a hostel in Westminster Bridge Road where she took up with a married, street-performing strong man by the name of Dixie Din. Their relationship was turbulent, to say the least. Dixie Din earned £3 a day entertaining theatre queues (a significant amount of money at the time), but he was hot-tempered and had threatened, on one occasion, to 'smash her face in'. Barbara had been to Davidson for help and the 5ft 3 in. rector had put on his clerical collar and gone in search of Din. He told him that he was a clergyman, that he was Barbara's uncle and politely asked him, in Barbara's words, not 'to bash in her face'. Mr Din clearly had a soft side, according to the rector's account, and Barbara confirmed that he had agreed to leave her alone.

Barbara told the court that she often stayed in Davidson's room when he was away, and sometimes when he was there as well. Davidson's landlady was not amused, Barbara said, not least when Davidson hammered on the door at one in the morning to get her to open up.

There was much comment after the lunch adjournment when Barbara retook the stand. She had changed her hat from the emerald green straw number of the previous day to a black silk skullcap. Levy asked her if it was new – she replied that it wasn't, although it *was* a clear sign that Barbara was enjoying the limelight and wanted to look her best for the assembled press. Levy went on to question her about her visit to the Stiffkey rectory. Davidson had given her ten shillings, part of which she used to buy a bathing costume. What irked her, she said, was that she had gone to Norfolk as a guest but had ended up working in the rectory kitchen without pay, with very little to eat and with only an invalid-chair to sleep on.

When she and Rose finally made it back to London, Barbara went straight to the Macfarlane Road house where she found Davidson about to depart for Stiffkey. Davidson was furious with her for leaving the rectory but finally agreed to help her find other employment. She had two brief and unsatisfactory spells working as a lady's maid; firstly with Lady Paget-Cooke and subsequently with one of his friends, Lady Waechter of Chiddingfold. Davidson then found her a job as a receptionist with a dentist in Euston Square but, when Levy probed, she revealed that this experience too had been problematic. The dentist's wife suspected her of kissing her husband and had assaulted her and Davidson had paid daily, uninvited visits to the surgery. It was agreed that Barbara would sleep at the surgery during the week and at Macfarlane Road at weekends while Davidson was away at his parish, but the rector's habit of staying in London on Saturday night and returning on the first train on Monday mornings meant that they ended up sharing the room for at least part of the week.

Under cross-examination by the defence the rather salacious tone of Davidson's visit with Barbara to Mrs Betty Beach became muted. Barbara conceded that she and Mrs Beach, the latter in her nightgown, did exercises together in front of the rector because they wanted to see if she would make it as a dancer. Barbara and the rector appear to have argued incessantly. On one occasion, alluded to by Barbara during her cross-examination, he had locked her in his room and on another she had given him a black eye.

Levy again pushed her to admit that she had suffered from venereal disease – to show that Davidson could not possibly have been interested in her in any sexual way – but she was immovable. The doctor at St George's Hospital, she said, had told her she was free of the disease. Levy went on to refer to Davidson's unusual habit of kissing and putting his arm around people he met, even if they were strangers. Barbara agreed with Levy's description of the rector as 'rather different from other people' but, as far as his touchy-feely manner was concerned, her response was, yet again, both to the point and damning:

'I have only seen it with girls.'

Levy went on to refer to a letter she wrote to Davidson on 20 October 1931, introduced in court as an exhibit (and pivotal to the story). In the letter Barbara writes affectionately to 'Uncle Harold' and asks him to help find a skin specialist for her sister. The tone of the letter suggests that Davidson had helped bring about a reconciliation between the two girls.

On 31 March Barbara took the stand for the third day. Once again, the national newspapers reported every detail of the story on their front pages. The regional *Eastern Daily Press* covered the story in great detail, omitting only the more spicy aspects of the case. Barbara's third day of evidence is covered in their 1 April edition and describes her as smartly dressed, pale but fully in control of her faculties. During re-examination, Oliver began by alluding to the defence suggestion that Rose Ellis had been bribed by Searle's agents to implicate the rector. Barbara had, he pointed out, written her letter of complaint to the Bishop of Norwich on 9 February; *before* Searle had interviewed her and she could not therefore have been induced to write it. The letter was produced as an exhibit, and read to the court. Written in neat, childlike block letters on fourteen pages of lined foolscap, it accuses the rector of a litany of misdemeanours including sexual misconduct, perjury, gross hypocrisy, passing dud cheques, and neglect of both his parish and his family. It constituted the most damning of all of the evidence produced against Davidson and from that point on the defence would face a difficult task to extricate the rector from the charges he was facing. Barbara's evidence to the court during the preceding two days had reiterated much of what she had written in the letter. It paints a stark picture (if its contents are to be believed) of a man who is out of control: Harold Davidson running around London entertaining teenage girls and buying them extravagant gifts while his family are 'starveing [*sic*] and had no coals'; Harold Davidson adopting the guise of a kindly priest to ingratiate himself with vulnerable teenage girls and Harold Davidson left embittered and isolated by an unfaithful wife. Harold Davidson stood at the helm of a leaking ship, kept afloat by large numbers of bounced cheques, by endless empty promises and (when he needed to cover his tracks), by lies and manipulation.

There is a tantalising (if inconclusive) reference to Barbara having been made pregnant by her Indian police officer boyfriend. During Roland Oliver's re-examination after her letter is produced, he asks her: 'When you were fifteen and a half you were got into trouble by this coloured man?' – 'Yes.'

It emerges, too, that her predicament made worse the already strained relationship that existed between Barbara and her family. Her sister Sylvia thoroughly disapproved of her, her brother refused to have her in his house and her mother, whom she had not seen for three years, was confined to a psychiatric hospital in Eastbourne.

After nine hours and twenty-five minutes of questioning over three days, the *Eastern Daily Press* reporter observed that Barbara was exhausted and seemed very relieved when she was allowed to stand down. Sylvia Harris, Barbara's sister, was the next to take the stand. Aged twenty-two and working as a maid, Sylvia told the court that Davidson had come to see her to suggest a reconciliation with Barbara, whom she had not seen for two and a half years. They had all met at the Macfarlane Road house but Davidson then appears to have focused his attentions on Sylvia, despite the fact that she had a fiancé. She testified that he had begun to 'pester' her, showing up at her place of employment on Armistice night in full uniform and medals, and writing her notes. The last time she saw him was at Baron's Court Tube station just before the scandal broke. He said to her, 'Before God I swear I am innocent.' Sylvia was unimpressed, telling Davidson that she knew he was in love with Barbara, as she had heard him call her 'Queen of My Heart'.

During the cross-examination Sylvia made it abundantly clear that she thoroughly disapproved of both her sister and Davidson. She believed, initially, that Davidson was trying to return Barbara's life to the straight and narrow, and had written to thank him for his efforts:

> My dear Padre,
>
> We thank you so much for our outing yesterday, also for the great trouble you must have taken over her for the results shown, I am proud she looks so well and so beautifully dressed. I felt so drab beside her.
>
> I have never had a happier day to finish up so well. I intend looking after her even if the rest of the family do not approve.
>
> It's funny how a small turning alters one's life. I am so glad you called Saturday...
>
> I am so proud to have a friend like you if I may say so.
>
> Yours affectionately,
>
> SYLVIA
>
> P.S. I am sure Barbara will realise and thank you one day.[10]

Sylvia soon began to suspect that he was interested in more than Barbara's soul, however. Levy failed utterly to shake her account of Davidson's behaviour and her remarks during Roland Oliver's re-examination were devastating to the defence case:

> Oliver: You came to what conclusion about Mr Davidson and your sister?
> Sylvia: I thought he must be in love with her.
> Oliver: Did you approve of that relationship?
> Sylvia: No.
> Chancellor North: Did you know he was a married man?
> Sylvia: Yes, he told me.
> Oliver: Why have you now abandoned her?
> Sylvia: Because I think she is not moral. I feel ashamed of her. I told her that I would help her as long as she had nothing more to do with him. She told me she had left him and then the next I heard was that she had gone back to Macfarlane Road.

The prosecution next called Percy Malyon, Sylvia's fiancé of three

---

10 Written in 1931 (exact date illegible). Included in the court papers at the Norfolk Record Office.

years. He was uncomfortable, he told the court, with the rector's over-familiarity with Sylvia and also with the tone of the letters that she had received from him. He recalled one outing when Davidson had put his arm through Sylvia's in a way that he thought to be 'very strange'.

Major Philip Hamond was called next, and he clearly relished the opportunity to inflict further damage on the rector's reputation. His evidence was brief – he confirmed to the court that it was customary for the Stiffkey parish priest to attend the annual Armistice commemoration but that Davidson had been absent from the November 1931 ceremony. This must have damned the rector in the eyes of many who had previously been sympathetic to him.

A chemist (the brother of the dentist for whom Barbara had worked, and one of those who had lost money to one of the Gordon scams) gave a rather benign account of Davidson's eccentricity, describing him as 'a very unconventional man'. He was undoubtedly tactile and over-familiar, the witness said, but in the ten years that he had known the rector he had never seen any behaviour that had gone beyond mild flirtation. This was a theme echoed by many of the witnesses. Mary Jane Bevan, the landlady of Barbara's Alderney Street bedsit, thought that Davidson was her uncle and had allowed him to visit her room. Barbara's room had no lock on the door and Miss Bevan neither suspected nor saw any sign of improper behaviour between them.

The last witness of the day was Barbara's landlady at Tolmer's Square, Euston, where she had lived with the Indian police officer during the last months of 1930. She recalled that Davidson had visited them both, but she reserved particular disdain for Barbara. When the Indian man had returned home in January 1931 Barbara had moved for a brief period into a cheaper room at the same address but the witness had asked her to leave when she brought men back to her room.

The trial moved into its fourth day, 1 April, with the defence and prosecution clashing repeatedly; with allegations of impropriety and witness-tampering from both sides. Public interest in the case was rising and the press described a stampede for seats as soon the doors of Church House were opened.

A Miss Violet Lowe, a waitress at the Yeng Wah Chinese Restaurant in Bloomsbury, was called first. She told the court that Davidson came in about three times a week and that she had seen the rector argue with Barbara and then put his arms around her and kiss her. She was asked

how long the embrace had lasted but she was unable to say. Attempts
by the prosecution to show that Davidson had made advances to Miss
Lowe were a conspicuous failure.

Levy requested that the defence's cross-examination of Miss Lowe be
deferred until he had received instructions from the rector. Oliver interjected, saying that he did not want her to be approached outside of
court by anyone from the defence team. He claimed that 'witness after
witness on our side has been interviewed'. Levy was outraged and
insisted that 'no witness for the prosecution has been interviewed by
anybody on behalf of Mr Davidson ever since this case began to be
heard in this court'. Oliver stuck to his guns, claiming that witnesses
subpoenaed by the prosecution had been approached by the defence.
Reading between the lines, it would appear that the person doing the
approaching was Davidson himself but the matter was left unresolved –
though the Chancellor issued a stern warning.

The Bishop of Norwich's legal counsel, Henry Dashwood of the firm
of Lee, Bolton and Lee, was called. He gave evidence relating to correspondence and interviews with Davidson in January of that year. Dashwood confirmed that Davidson had confided that he was not the father
of his youngest child. Levy protested that the information had been
given in confidence but Roland Oliver replied 'It is a terrible thing to
produce, but it must be introduced in evidence to corroborate Barbara's
story.' Dashwood confirmed that Barbara had been paid various sums
of money by his law firm; it had provided most of her living expenses
during the weeks immediately before the trial. Levy accused the prosecution of buying her evidence, describing the payments as 'monstrous
and improper'. Chancellor North alluded to attempts made by the
defence (again, presumably by Davidson himself) to tamper with
Barbara. Levy was incensed by the allegation, and the two counsels
clashed again:

> Levy (addressing the Chancellor): I protest against what I consider
> to be a gradual and complete poisoning of your mind in this case.
> There has never been any attempt to tamper with Barbara Harris.
> Oliver: I am calling a great deal of evidence about attempts to
> tamper with Barbara Harris.

During Dashwood's evidence details emerged of the frequently
underhand methods employed by the bishop's agents to secure evidence

against the rector. Davidson was followed ceaselessly, as was Barbara, and Rose Ellis was harassed to the point where her mother instructed her solicitor to write a letter of complaint. In it Rose flatly refuses to appear in court:

If what is being done is being done in the name of the Church, all we can say is God help the Church, and it is little wonder that clergy are often complaining about the lack of public attendances in church. Miss Ellis rightly and properly resents being shadowed by private inquiry agents. We are so disgusted with the methods of the Church as they appear to us that we are not prepared to in any way further interest ourselves in this matter.[11]

Dashwood went on to confirm that during interviews with the rector he had urged him to resign. At one meeting he had told him:

You are in a big hole, and for the sake of your wife I have asked you to come here. I want you to go to your solicitor and tell him what you have been doing in London in the last six months and seek his advice, always having regard to your children whether to resign your living forthwith and submit to the Bishop of Norwich, whom you trust, or whether to go into public court, which you know would damage your children forever.

The prosecution now turned to address the second charge and called Dorothy Burn, a blonde twenty-one-year-old manageress to a corset-maker, who had been, in the summer of 1929, a waitress at a Lyons teahouse in Walbrook, in the City of London. She told the court that Davidson had become a regular customer and developed a fixation on her, following her around the shop and telling her she was lovely and far too good to be working in a teahouse. He invited her to tea and to spend the weekend at the Stiffkey rectory but she was unimpressed – in her words, 'I did not like him. He used to pester me.' Davidson told her on one occasion that when she married he would perform the ceremony and that she 'would have eight children'. This last remark provoked a burst of laughter in court, with Davidson joining in, but the Chancellor quickly issued a rebuke.

---

11 Letter from the Ellis family solicitors, quoted in the *Eastern Daily Press* of 2 April 1932.

Miss Burn said that the 'pestering' went on for two months and that Davidson had once followed her down to the ladies' cloakroom before being ejected by the manageress. Davidson was interviewed by a Lyons investigator and effectively barred from the Walbrook branch, but showed up again the next day and sat writing while his male companion was served. Levy cross-examined Miss Burn, arguing that Davidson was merely a harmless eccentric who had made his remarks to her in full view of a restaurant full of people. He also defended the rector's suggestion that Miss Burn visit the Stiffkey rectory but the levity of her reply did nothing to soften its impact on Davidson's tottering reputation:

> Levy: There could be no harm in going to a clergyman's house where his wife and children were living, could there?
> Miss Burn: I don't know. I would not like to chance it. (Laughter.)

Levy also made the point that Davidson's comment that she was too good to be a waitress had been proved to be accurate. She was now manageress to a corset-maker, he told her, but before she could reply her mother stood up and shouted, 'She did not get the job through him either! He made her ill!'

Frederick Stevens, chief inquiry officer of Lyons and Company, was the last witness of the day. He corroborated Miss Burn's account, telling the court that after a complaint about the rector's behaviour at the Walbrook teahouse he had stopped Davidson in the street outside and told him that he was barred from the premises. Davidson's reaction had been typical: he told Stevens, 'Certainly, I will go to the ABC or the Express where I am well known.' Laughter again erupted at this and Chancellor North threatened to clear the court. Stevens had told Davidson that if he came in again that he would not be served but, true to form, on the following day he had done exactly that.[12] Davidson also threatened to sue J. Lyons and Company, telling Stevens that he knew nearly all of the firm's directors and had already been awarded £200 for a previous assault by one of their staff. Levy suggested that the company disliked the rector because he had tried to improve the working conditions of the girls but Stevens denied this. He said that the real problem was that Davidson simply would not leave the girls alone:

12 See Dorothy Burn's evidence above.

Oliver: What was Lyons' objection to Mr Davidson?

Stevens: His behaviour towards the waitresses. He used to pester them, follow them about, and ask them to go to theatres, particularly the young girls. I know of instances where he has asked them to go to theatres, even *trippies*[13]... In one shop in St James's that has happened and he is known there among the waitresses as 'the Mormon'.

The case entered its fifth day on Saturday 2 April. Rose Ellis's boyfriend was called, a young driver whose name was withheld from the court.[14] He recalled an evening in January when Davidson had visited the rooms that he and Rose shared. Davidson asked her what she had said to the bishop's agents and why she had done it. She told him that she had supplied a thirteen-page statement detailing her relationship with him. Davidson was so distressed that he threatened to jump under a train but Rose eventually agreed to go to a solicitor and sign an affidavit retracting her statement.

Mrs Ada Woodford, Rose's landlady, testified that Davidson would visit her tenant at all hours of the day or night. Davidson's ability to last for days without sleep is mentioned many times throughout the trial and is yet another facet of his extraordinary personality. Mrs Woodford often saw him spend an hour or two napping in an armchair and then carry on as if he had had a full night's rest. Davidson had told her that Rose was deeply troubled. She had unwittingly entered into a bigamous marriage with an army officer who turned out to have four children, she had attempted suicide twice and was prone to hysterical fits that Mrs Woodford had witnessed herself. Rose also lived, like Davidson, in permanent expectation of a financial windfall from the elusive Mr Gordon. In Rose's case she was expecting £5,000, said Mrs Woodford. Under cross-examination, Mrs Woodford said that despite Davidson's eccentricities, 'I never thought anything but that he was a gentleman.'

Davidson's fondness for a pretty face seemed to know no bounds, and his behaviour was often reckless beyond belief. A pretty young woman in a long black fur-trimmed coat took the stand. Kathleen Edith Grant (née Pritchard), twenty-three years old and recently married, was

13 Young girls between sixteen and eighteen training to become waitresses, or 'nippies'.
14 In fact it was Billy Parsloe, described in some accounts as her fiancé.

no ordinary Lyons waitress. Her mother lived in Stiffkey and Davidson first met her before she married when she had come to the village church. In 1930 she was living in the room subsequently taken over by Barbara Harris, in Providence Place, Shepherd's Bush. Davidson began to visit the teahouse where she worked and asked her to go the theatre with him.

As always with Davidson it was never quite clear what his true intentions were – whether he was simply being friendly or whether he expected more – but there is no doubt that, at the very least, his behaviour was bizarre. He showed up at her lodgings at 12 o'clock at night, claiming to have a message from her mother. Her mother subsequently denied this, telling Kathleen that Davidson had badgered her relentlessly until she gave him the address. Kathleen refused to go out for coffee, telling him she was tired and Davidson left.

He then embarked, according to her evidence, on a 'pestering' routine that was by now familiar to the court. In her case he told her he could get her into films because 'she had wonderful eyes', talked to her incessantly while she was serving other customers and pursued her to the point where she would hide behind a pillar when he came in. What was going on in Davidson's head? Under cross-examination Kathleen confirmed that the rector 'never at any time made anything like an improper suggestion' to her, but perhaps it points to a voyeuristic streak in him or possibly an addiction to risk.

The next witness was Mrs Lake, Barbara Harris's landlady. She had been taken ill and so, in astonishing scenes, the entire Consistory Court travelled in a cavalcade of cars to Shepherd's Bush to interview her in bed. On the day of the visit, there were crowds lining the streets, hoping for a glimpse of the notorious rector, and police reinforcements had to be summoned to clear a path to the house. Mrs Lake's statement was taken and was read to the court the following Monday.

That Sunday, 3 April, Davidson conducted the morning service in Stiffkey church. He was now a national, even an international, celebrity and the press reported every detail of his movements. The trial was far from over but among the accounts of that Sunday there is a common thread – a sense of something akin to a valediction. Davidson travelled from Norwich on Saturday night, arriving at Norwich station at 2 am and sleeping in an armchair in the waiting room for a few hours before cadging a lift in a van for the remainder of his journey. When he emerged from the rectory dressed for the morning service at Stiffkey church, he was greeted by a small crowd of parishioners and posed for a press photographer. The church was decorated for Easter with primroses and daffodils and Davidson stood stiffly in the pulpit, wearing his three war medals.

After a hymn the congregation of about fifty souls were asked to pray, 'on behalf of everyone of those interested or affected by this case – those giving evidence and those affected by the evidence'. Before the collection he announced that after taking the usual amount from the tray for the parish, he would donate the remainder to help 'some of the poor girls in London whom I have not been able to help very much just lately'. At the end of the lesson a press photographer leapt up to take a photo but was asked by Davidson to wait until the service was over.

The afternoon service was at Morston church, which was packed. After it ended Davidson stood at the porch shaking hands with almost every member of the congregation as they filed out. This pattern was repeated during evensong at Stiffkey. People had come from all of the surrounding districts; there was even a coach-party from Norwich; and two policemen were on hand to control the crowds. The choice of hymns was surely significant: 'O God, our help in ages past', 'Rock of ages' and 'Abide with me'. When the service ended Davidson left for Norwich where he caught the night train to London.

During the sixth day of evidence, Monday 4 April, Roland Oliver began by reading out the statement taken from Alice Lake the previous Saturday. Mrs Lake's statement corroborated Kathleen Grant's account of Davidson's nocturnal visits to her flat in Providence Place, and described how he brought Barbara Harris to take over the tenancy when the girl moved out. Davidson came to see Barbara at inappropriate times, often late at night and sometimes with other young women in tow. Mrs Lake or her husband were constantly turning Davidson away from Barbara's door but he continued to come, right up to the time that the two women had received subpoenas. On his last visit Davidson had told her that he was facing six months in prison and wanted to keep Barbara out of the affair. He had also told Mrs Lake, just as Roland Oliver had claimed in his opening remarks, that Barbara had been in Holloway prison; the implication being that the rector had been attempting to 'nobble' the prosecution's star witness. Mrs Lake's husband had eventually told her to eject him from the house.

Ryder Richardson, one of Davidson's defence counsel, had subjected Mrs Lake to a bedside cross-examination. She agreed with the description of Barbara as an immature young woman who liked to stay in bed all morning and whom Davidson had bailed out financially on a number of occasions. Barbara was also something of a fantasist:

Ryder Richardson: Did not Barbara say that she was keen on getting into a murder trial?
Mrs Lake: Not a murder trial. She said a big trial. She said that she did not mind her photograph getting into the papers. She wanted something thrilling to happen to her.

Rose Ellis's boyfriend, the young unnamed driver who had given evidence on Saturday, was cross-examined next. He told Levy that Searle's agents had paid her small sums of money, totalling £2 in all, to cooperate with the investigation and had also bought her a new coat. Rose had also told him that Searle had plied her with six or seven glasses of port and had told her that they were simply trying to jolt Davidson into spending more time in his parish instead of in London.

Levy read out a letter written by Rose to a friend called Miss Short, identified in court as 'Miss S'. It contained a declaration that she planned to retract the statements she had made to Searle and his men:

Dear Miss Short – It was very kind of you to send a message to me saying you have a dress for me. I will come along tonight for it with a boyfriend of mine. When I come I want you very much to do a little favour. Foolishly I made a mistake under considerable temptation which has placed a mutual friend of ours in a very terrible position and most unjustly so. I want to put it right if I possibly can and a journalist friend of mine advises me to write a true statement which would do so. I will bring it with me and I want you to witness my signature to it and then perhaps you will send it for me.[15]

Just as there are anomalies in Barbara Harris's letter to the Bishop of Norwich, there is a distinctly fishy aroma about this missive as well. The defence seized upon it as proof of a plot by the prosecution to get

15 Letter from Rose Ellis to a Miss Short, dated 25 January 1932 and included in the court papers at the Norfolk Record Office.

Davidson convicted at all costs but the fact that Rose Ellis, described by Davidson himself as 'slow witted', could write so eloquently must raise a suspicion that she was coached. The first sentence is, in fact, exactly what one would expect Rose to have written but the rest is uncharacteristic, to say the least.

Next up was Mrs Flora Osborne, Davidson's former landlady at Barnard Street, Russell Square. Mrs Osborne turned out to be a formidable witness for the prosecution – she had known Davidson for four years and clearly thought very little of him. He had first rented a room from her in 1928 and was constantly in arrears, she said. She had given him notice to quit on half a dozen occasions and had taken out six court summonses against him for non-payment of rent. He was always bringing young women back to his room, she said, telling her that they were part of his 'rescue work'. The most frequent visitor was 'Mrs Malone', which was Rose Ellis's pseudonym, whom Davidson claimed to be his secretary. Mrs Osborne had hired three of the girls as maids but 'did not think much of them'.

Her description of a trip to Stiffkey in 1928 provides a telling example of Davidson's rashness and eccentricity. She and her husband drove up to Norfolk with Davidson and a young woman called Winifred Wayne, a clergyman's daughter who was later to become a nun, but at the time the leading actress at London's Regent Theatre.[16] At one point during the return journey Mrs Osborne turned round to see Davidson in the back seat with his arm around Miss Wayne. When they reached London, she said, Davidson had gone to his room with her. Their stay at the rectory was captured in a bizarre photograph taken in the grounds (illustration 19). It shows Davidson, Mrs Osborne and the young actress with what appears to be a boy hiding behind a shrub. In fact it was Davidson's wife Molly, who disliked having her picture taken.

Mrs Osborne described one occasion when Davidson, in arrears as usual with his rent, was preparing to take a bath. She had given Davidson an eviction notice the week before but the rector had ignored it. She climbed in through the bathroom window just as he was undressing and took hold of him. Her husband had to intervene to separate them

16 Winifred Wayne was already an accomplished actress when this incident occurred. She played leading roles in Martin Sabine's repertory company including, in December 1926, the lead in the show *Daddy Long Legs*. The National Portrait Gallery's collections include four portraits of Miss Wayne.

but she still managed to eject the unfortunate rector from the house. Under cross-examination by Levy, she conceded that she had a ferocious temper and that her husband had threatened 'a hundred and one times' to go abroad to get away from her. Levy's attempts to portray Davidson as a meddling but well-intentioned fool were abruptly rebuffed:

> Levy: It is a fact that a maid named Lizzie was taken ill?
>
> Mrs Osborne (interjecting): Oh, so that has come. My God. Yes she was taken ill with appendicitis.
>
> Levy: Did not Mr Davidson help and bring an ambulance?
>
> Mrs Osborne: There are two things Mr Davidson has done in my life and that is one... I asked him to get into his clerical clothes and go for an ambulance, and I had to give him five shillings to take a taxi. The only two things he has done in my life were to get something for my nerves and to get an ambulance for Lizzie. He even remembers that. What a charming man!

Another landlady, a Mrs Jordan of Euston Street, had let a room to Davidson and gave evidence of the stream of waifs and strays, all young and all female, who beat a path to his door. Rose Ellis (known to the witness as 'Mrs Malone') was a constant visitor. Mrs Jordan thought little of the girls and thought even less of the fact that they were entertained by the rector in his room but, as with the other landladies, no evidence of any sexual activity was forthcoming.

Tuesday 5 April was day seven of the trial. Chancellor North told the court that he had received a number of anonymous letters protesting about the press reporting details of the trial and demanding that it be held *in camera*. North said that he had no powers to order that the trial be held in secret and it was important that the actions of the court be subjected to scrutiny.

Details of Davidson's 1925 bankruptcy were provided by the day's first witness, Charles Prior, the Official Receiver for Norwich. Davidson was still undischarged and had seen his living reduced from £800 a year to about £400 to pay off his creditors.

The spectre of Barbara's sexual promiscuity was raised once again by the next witness. Dr Francis Doble of Harley Street told the court that Barbara's symptoms were not unlike those associated with venereal disease but that she did not actually have it. Barbara herself was then called for further cross-examination by Levy. She was questioned about Dixie Din, the married street-performing strong man with whom she had taken up in May 1931. The defence, presumably acting on what Dixie Din had told them, asked Barbara if it was true that during their rendezvous in the Cosy Café on Edgware Road she had sat on his knee and tried to undo his clothes. Barbara flatly denied that she had done this, and also denied that she had been trying to get the brawny boulevardier to pay her for sex.

Two more landladies followed Barbara onto the stand, one critical of the rector and the other not. The first described how she had caught him in a darkened room with a young girl called Nellie Churchill. She gave Davidson a good telling off, but he responded that the gas had gone out. Miss Churchill, she said, was now confined in an asylum, although there was no suggestion that Davidson was in any way responsible for her predicament.

The staff of various ABC cafés seemed to have had the same disdain for Davidson as their colleagues at the Lyons teahouses. Miss Phyllis Holt, one of their waitresses, painted a picture of the rector as an out-and-out pest whom the girls would avoid. He would ask her out to the cinema and sometimes showed her two theatre tickets, leaving one under a plate for her. She always turned him down, she said, as did Winifred Barker, another waitress who told the court that the rector had patted her under the chin and admired her teeth. Three ABC inquiry officers were called next – all testifying that Davidson was regarded as a nuisance who had been the subject of so many complaints by female staff members that he had eventually been barred from the company's restaurants.

Davidson's pile of problems continued to grow on the following day, Wednesday 6 April, when Richard Levy announced that the funds for the rector's defence were almost exhausted. He predicted that within one or two days Davidson would be left without legal representation and would have to defend himself. Later in the day the prosecution unexpectedly offered to put up £250 to allow his defence lawyers to continue to represent him and, if necessary, to consider advancing more funds or to agree to an adjournment. During the lunchtime adjournment Davidson told a reporter that he had already spent between £500 and £700 on his defence. He hailed the generosity of his friends and supporters but also referred to his desperate attempts to raise funds: 'I have not been to bed since last Thursday night, for I have been busy writing articles and my life story in order to raise money. I estimate that taking all possible contingencies into account I shall require about another £1,500.'[17]

Oliver and Levy both addressed the court during the day and it was eventually agreed that, at the conclusion of the case for the prosecution, the court would adjourn until 19 May to give Davidson time to raise more funds. (In his 1934 pamphlet *The Reason Why*, written two years after the conclusion of the trial, Davidson is especially bitter about the amount spent by the Bishop of Norwich to prosecute the case. The official figure, given in answer to a parliamentary question, was £8,205 – quadruple the amount spent on the trial of the mass-murderer Dr Crippen.)

The next witness to be called was Christopher John Searle, the investigator from the Arrow's Detective Agency. Searle described his meetings with Rose Ellis and flatly denied that he had plied her with port, or otherwise bribed her to incriminate Davidson. He also refuted the suggestion that he pretended to Rose that he was from a charitable agency that provided assistance to out of work young women, and disputed her allegation that they had said they were simply trying to jolt Davidson into spending more time in his parish. What he did concede was that, of the dozens of women interviewed for the trial, Rose was the only person to suggest that they had had sexual intercourse. Barbara's many and varied allegations against the rector stopped just short of suggesting this.

Inglebert Thole and Percy Butler, two of Searle's colleague at Arrow's, were called next. Both had shadowed Davidson on different days during the months of July and October 1931. What emerges from their almost balletic pursuit of the rector across London was not that he spent his days leaping in and out of beds, but that large parts of his life consisted of more or less unabated pointlessness and dissipation. The snapshots they provide are of Harold Davidson smoking large numbers of sixpenny cigars (or simply holding an unlighted butt in his characteristically theatrical way), of Harold Davidson whiling away the afternoons in an ABC or Lyons teahouse with Barbara or Rose or Mrs Beach, of Harold Davidson sitting in a theatre matinée with Barbara

---

17 Quoted in the *Eastern Daily Press*, 7 April 1932.

courtesy of one of his many gratis tickets, and of Harold Davidson on the London Underground squabbling with Barbara or trying to chat up yet another young woman with his interminable 'Has anyone told you that you resemble ——?' lines. He seemed to know everyone and everyone knew him. In one memorable incident Percy Butler followed him to the Marquis of Cornwallis pub near Russell Square. Not for Davidson the respectful greeting from his grateful flock. The landlord shouted 'Hello, you old thief. Still getting cash. How are all the girls?' Davidson cashed two cheques at the bar and raced off to take Barbara shopping.

The prosecution's case was concluded on Thursday 7 April. Davidson rejected the prosecution's offer of £250 towards his defence on the basis that he did not wish 'to be under any sense of obligation' to them. Chancellor North was under the impression that the money was to come from the Ecclesiastical Commissioners but Oliver was non-committal and, in the end, the rector decided that he would try to raise funds from other sources or conduct his own defence. It was agreed that Davidson could continue to conduct services in Stiffkey so long as he did not refer to the case – or 'disseminate propaganda' as Oliver put it – and the hearing was adjourned until Thursday 19 May.

5
The Rector Takes the Stand

On 8 April, the day after the court adjourned, Harold Davidson put out a public appeal for donations to his defence fund. The appeal was carried in a number of newspapers with Davidson quoted as saying that he was flat broke. His friends, Lady Waechter among them, stepped forward and by the time the case resumed in May he and his defence team were in fighting form.

When he opened the case for the defence on 19 May, Richard Levy spoke before a packed court for more than five hours. What the case came down to, he said, was that there was only one piece of direct evidence against Davidson and that was the testimony of Barbara Harris. Davidson had helped 'not one young woman, not a dozen, not twenty, but hundreds of young women', Levy said, and yet, he continued, 'Among all these women not one has come forward in this case to say that Mr. Davidson had had relations with her.' Because they lacked any credible evidence beyond the word of Barbara Harris, the prosecution resorted to 'suspicion, suggestion, insinuation, and prejudice' to advance their case against the rector. They 'created an atmosphere of suspicion and distortion in which nothing could be presented in true normal and ordinary conditions, but everything, however innocent, assumed an appearance of distortion and guilt as though one were looking in a distorting mirror'. To prove his point Levy cited the example of Mrs Betty Beach, named in the fourth charge as one of the 'women of a loose character' with whom Davidson had associated. There had not been, he said, a shred of evidence to besmirch the virtue and reputation of Mrs Beach and yet the prosecution had allowed, even encouraged, the press to drag her name through the mud.

Similarly, there was no compelling evidence to support the second charge, relating to the Lyons waitress Dorothy Burn. It was clear that Davidson had annoyed the girl, and many others too, said Levy. Further, Davidson insisted on talking to people about themselves, and telling them everything about himself. There was no doubt that the rector was 'a troublesome busybody', said Levy, but this did not mean that he made, as the charge stated, 'improper suggestions' to Miss Burn.

Levy reserved his most scathing criticisms for Henry Dashwood, legal counsel to the Bishop of Norwich, who had 'created an atmosphere of guilt before the case was ever launched'. Dashwood had 'issued a perfect wave of subpoenas right and left upon everybody connected or concerned with the case' and had then told the defence that they could not interview any of these people or even approach them until the case came to court. This made it impossible, Levy said, to prepare an adequate defence. Levy went on to say that 'This matter was conceived in obstinate ignorance, launched in venom and spite, and carried on to the very end in spite and in persecution.' He said it was incredible that the prosecution had not called Rose Ellis, the subject of the most serious of the charges against Davidson. He was accused of conducting an adulterous relationship with Rose for a decade and the charge was clearly based on her initial statement to the bishop's agents and yet, when she retracted her statement, the prosecution had stepped aside and told the defence that they could call her as their own witness if they wished to.

Davidson was a kissing fool, said Levy. He kissed his landlady, his landlady's daughters, his maids, and most of his female acquaintances when they looked sad or when he was simply saying goodbye to them. Davidson's kissing, like much of his behaviour, 'might give wrong impressions to the suspicious mind because he is so utterly and completely unconventional and thoughtless as to the appearance of anything he does'. For thirty years, instead of 'sitting in the richer drawing rooms of his parish and taking tea with ladies', he had helped hundreds of girls to escape poverty, homelessness and the lure of prostitution. Barbara Harris was 'only one of legions but was the one who has turned and bitten the hand that has fed her'.

Levy said it was highly significant that the only one of Davidson's landladies not to have been called was Mrs Jessie Walton, owner of the house in Macfarlane Road, Shepherd's Bush, where Davidson was alleged to have conducted affairs with both Barbara Harris and Rose Ellis. In fact, he said, the defence would call Mrs Walton and she would nail, once and for all, the lie that Davidson had ever slept in the same room as Barbara. Whenever Davidson slept at the house Barbara would sleep downstairs in Mrs Walton's daughter's room. Mrs Walton, like Rose Ellis, had not been called by the prosecution because they were interested only in those witnesses who would further their case. Difficult witnesses or those whose testimony contradicted the prosecution case were simply excluded from the trial.

Chancellor North interjected to ask if the defence intended to call Rose. Levy replied that they would not. 'The burden is not upon me to disprove these charges,' he said, and the case was thus refined to a simple choice: was Barbara believable or would the rector, when he took the stand during the coming days, succeed in dispelling the cloud of suspicion that floated above his head? Levy dismissed Barbara Harris as a fantasist who was 'living not in a world of truth and fact but in a world of fancy and imagination created by herself, instilled perhaps by the distorted sort of life she has had to live and by the innumerable detective stories which she is so fond of reading'. Throughout the trial there had been drama and conflict, but in even the most casual study of the court transcripts one can detect that the tension had, at this stage, become heightened, there was a sense that matters were coming to a climax. Levy had spoken for five hours and the court was adjourned until the following day.

Harold Davidson entered the witness-box on Friday 20 May. The court was packed – people queued right down the street to see the old actor take the stage for the part of his life and they were not disappointed. He took the oath and then sat beside Chancellor North, just as Barbara Harris had done during the prosecution phase. Davidson was examined by Ryder Richardson, who got straight to the point:

> Richardson: Have you ever been guilty of immorality?
> Davidson: No.
> Richardson: Have you lived in adultery with any woman?
> Davidson: No.
> Richardson: Have you ever importuned a woman with immoral intent?
> Davidson: Never in my life.

He was asked how many girls he had helped and the number he gave, 'between 500 and 1,000', though far less than the '150 to 200 girls a year' claimed in his pamphlet *The Reason Why*, was still remarkably large. He described how he had taken 'a great many girls' to Paris to train as domestic servants at the school run by his friend just outside the city. Rose had hated the school and was soon back living in London but he'd had more success with the others, he said.

Tom Cullen quotes J. Rowland Sales (who attended the trial) as saying that throughout the first day Davidson was very much the respectable country parson; his responses were polite, restrained and measured. On the second day, however, Saturday 21 May, it was a different person that entered the box. Chancellor North ticked him off almost immediately for fidgeting and sitting with his hands in his pockets, to which Ryder Richardson commented: 'I am afraid you are asking the impossible. I do not think that Mr Davidson has ever remained in one position for more than five minutes in his life. But I hope you will not think that he is acting from wilful malice.'

Davidson claimed that Mrs Osborne did not object to his taking girls back to his rooms. Rose came to see him about once a week, he agreed, but Mrs Osborne made no fuss about her, or about the other girls he brought to his room as late as 11 o'clock at night. Mrs Osborne was rather less cordial when she was in her cups, he said: 'It was only when she had a little too much to drink that she became very unpleasant with everybody.'

He flatly denied Mrs Osborne's claim that he'd had his arm around a young actress called Winifred Wayne in the back of their car as they drove him back from a weekend at the Stiffkey vicarage in 1928. She was the daughter of a friend of his, a New Zealand clergyman. At the time of the car journey she was thinking of converting to Roman Catholicism and Davidson was doing his best to dissuade her, he said. He had hoped to invite the Bishop of Norwich to tea at the vicarage during the weekend and introduce the girl to him but in the event it did not happen. Davidson's somewhat glib answers to questions asked by his own counsel about his relationship with Miss Wayne almost got him into trouble with Chancellor North:

Richardson: It is alleged that you sat with your arm around the girl's waist in the car?
Davidson: No, certainly not.
Richardson: You cannot do that in a motorcar?
Davidson: Perhaps you and I hold different opinions as to that possibility.

Richardson: Did you?

Davidson: No, I did not.

Chancellor: Your counsel, Mr Richardson, knows what is good for you, far better than you do yourself. Just attend to him and answer his questions.

Davidson: This is all new to me.

Rose Ellis had been his secretary and no more, declared Davidson. She assisted with papers, sewed his clothes and (on one occasion) carried his bag. He met the mysterious Mr Gordon almost every day, usually in a Lyons teahouse or in one of the hotels, although the rector's almost complete inability to be on time meant that they would often miss each other. This was the reason, claimed Davidson, that he was always approaching teahouse waitresses: to ask them to pass messages to Gordon. He would always select a waitress who looked reliable and then attract her attention by putting his hand on her arm. He was always touching people for emphasis, he said, and meant nothing improper by it:

Richardson: Are you nervous in the use of your hands, and do you touch people?

Davidson: Yes, I often emphasise things like that. I had to restrain myself a moment ago from touching the Chancellor.

Chancellor: You had better not.

Given that there was no jury in this trial and that it would be the Chancellor who would decide Davidson's fate, some of the rector's replies were unbelievably flippant. The transcript of the trial, especially on this particular day, has the flavour of a comedy routine with the rector's counsel as 'straight man'. Davidson was questioned about his habit of stuffing papers and photographs in his pockets and money in the top of his socks. The Chancellor's frequent interjections suggest that he found the rector's behaviour to be bizarre in the extreme:

Richardson: Is it true to say your pockets are generally bulging with photographs and papers?

Davidson: Yes, I am the despair of my tailor. I had sixteen pockets put into this suit.

Richardson: Where do you keep your money?

Davidson: At that time I used to keep it in the top of my sock, but I do not want anyone to know that. (Laughter.)

Richardson: Is it true that you flourished money in front of the waitresses?

Davidson: No. I folded up one five pounds and put it in one sock and put the other five pounds in the other.

Chancellor: Did you do this in public?

Davidson: Yes, but not too publicly... It is the last place which a burglar would think of. I have so often had my pockets picked by pickpockets. Anyone who wanted to take it would have to take my boots off.

Richardson put it to Davidson that 'he was a man of impetuosities' and the rector agreed that he was. 'I never think whether a thing is advisable or not.... I go straight away and do it on the spur of the moment,' he said. He was always preaching to waitresses and theatre girls, sometimes backstage and on occasion while they were getting changed. He knew hundreds of Lyons girls and clearly did not endear himself to their employers when he campaigned for better wages for them during the years immediately after the First World War. In 1919 he had sued the firm after he was assaulted by one of their staff and been awarded £200. This, he said, was why the company had it in for him and why its staff were so eager to appear for the prosecution.

The issue of the parentage of Davidson's fifth child was raised again during the rector's evidence. When Ryder Richardson asked him if the story was true he responded that it was 'totally and absolutely untrue'. It had first become part of Stiffkey gossip around 1920 but Davidson insisted that he had actually returned home on leave in October 1918 for a few hours, the implication being that it was then that the child was conceived.[1] He had told Henry Dashwood about the existence of the rumour, *not* that the rumour was true, and had been assured that the prosecution would not mention it in court unless Davidson tried to use it as an excuse for being away in London so much. He was deeply upset by the fact that the prosecution had broken its promise: 'This is the only bitter feeling I have in this case, that this poor child should have to read about it in the newspaper from your opening statement, Mr Oliver.' Applause and murmured 'Hear, hears' were heard at the back of the

[1] This conflicts with the evidence of Davidson's naval records (see page 16).

court and in the gallery, much to the irritation of Chancellor North. He ordered that the gallery be cleared but immediately thought better of it and instead ordered one woman who had been particularly vocal to leave the court. Davidson was visibly overcome by the incident and was allowed to leave the court for a few minutes while he composed himself.

The court resumed with talk of Cairo brothels, a subject on which the rector professed himself to be something of an expert. He had told Barbara of his experiences in the hope, he said, that it would divert her from the life she was leading. Chancellor North sounded decidedly sceptical that Davidson's behaviour had been prudent:

> Chancellor: Did you introduce Barbara to your daughter knowing what Barbara is?
> Davidson: Yes, knowing what she might become.
> Chancellor: And Rose Ellis?
> Davidson: Yes, why not?

North asked for an explanation, to which Davidson responded: 'If you are going to make these girls outcasts forever, how can you hope to raise them up? You must get them among respectable people. The great failure of the Church is that the icebergs of chastity draw their skirts away from these girls.'

The case was adjourned until the following Monday, 23 May, the day beginning with questions about the unfortunate Nellie Churchill, once employed by Davidson as an artist's model and now afflicted with a mental disorder. All of Davidson's attempts to help her had come to nothing and she was now confined to a psychiatric hospital. When the landlady had discovered them together in the dark, explained Davidson, it was because the gas was not working and they were unable to light the lamps in her room. Groping around in the dark with Nellie Churchill was yet another example of Davidson being caught in a seemingly compromising situation with a young woman. He offered an innocent explanation once again, but the steady drip of aspersion and innuendo was taking its toll.

He was questioned about his habit of pressing theatre tickets on the young women he met and he said that at one stage he was giving away 150 tickets a week. He considered himself an authority on the theatre and believed that '99 per cent' of young women at some point dreamt of going on the stage. He had helped to produce a small number of films and had even gone to Waterloo Station at 1.30 in the morning with a group of friends to appear as an unpaid extra in a movie. He styled himself as a sort of unaffiliated talent scout, eternally on the lookout among London's womanhood for the 'Next Big Thing'. Winifred Barker was not the only girl to have her teeth inspected by the rector; he did it all the time, he said. Chancellor North was incredulous:

Chancellor: Do you say that you would pull her lip down and look at her teeth?
Davidson: Yes, if she were asking me if she were suitable for film work.
Chancellor: It is what you would do to a horse if you wanted to tell if it were below a certain age?
Davidson: Yes, but they were their assets.
Chancellor: Would you do it without her leave?
Davidson: Certainly not, only if she were asking me if she were suitable.

Richardson began to question Davidson about his relationship with Barbara Harris. He had indeed seen her talking to a notorious madam outside the Marble Arch Tube station and had gone over to warn her after the woman left. She became his 'adopted niece', an Irish custom learned from his wife. It was true that he had frequently visited her Alderney Street bedsit but had never wedged the door shut with a chair to prevent the landlady from entering. He emphatically denied that he had tried to rape Barbara, saying that the girl had tried to force herself upon him. He had arrived at her room one lunchtime to collect her and discovered that she was still in bed, suffering from a hangover:

Davidson: Naturally I was annoyed, especially as she told me she had been drunk the night before, and I suppose my voice showed it... Then she got out of bed and put both arms around me, and twined her legs in a most unpleasant way all round me, and kissed me in a most disgusting and offensive way. I threw her back on the bed and I said, 'Do not do that again.'
Richardson: Did she tell you what she was doing?
Davidson: She used the phrase 'I am making love with my legs'.

Richardson: What was your attitude to the incident?

Davidson: After that I never went back to the house again to see her. I apologised for having thrown her back on the bed before I left, because I did it very roughly perhaps...

Richardson: Did you ever say you wanted to possess her body and soul?

Davidson: No, I said I was ready to fight for her body and soul.

Richardson: Even a remark like that unexplained sounds extraordinary?

Davidson: One's whole career as a clergyman is fighting for people's souls, and very often their bodies. Very often you have to do the body first.

Davidson went on to issue a succession of categorical denials, contradicting Barbara's evidence more or less in its entirety: he had never been entertained to tea by Barbara and her Indian boyfriend in their pyjamas, had never said to her 'I would rather have you without them', and had never kept condoms in a trunk in his room. In fact, he said, he had never used a condom. He had also never used pyjamas: Barbara's claim that he had climbed in to bed with her wearing only a pyjama top was an outright lie, he said. To his recollection he had never had intercourse with his wife 'for any other purpose than the sacred purpose of procreating children' and he had never made love to his wife without praying first.

The rector was mystified by Barbara's detailed description of his appendicitis scar; clear evidence, if it can be believed, that they were intimate. He did not deny that he had one:

Richardson: Has Barbara Harris ever seen your stomach?

Davidson: Unless she peeped through the bathroom door, as she did through other doors sometimes, I think not.

Richardson: Has she ever with your knowledge and consent seen your stomach?

Davidson: Never.

Davidson had called Barbara 'Queen of My Heart' and the prosecution had suggested that this was proof that they were conducting an affair. In fact, Davidson said, he called everyone, including his landlady, 'Queen of My Heart'. The phrase came from the title of a popular song,

'You are Queen of My Heart'[2] and the rector applied the phrase to almost every women he befriended.

Ryder Richardson asked Davidson about Barbara's assertion that he helped only young women, but the rector replied that he had helped a great many young men, including three or four who had stayed at the rectory. He also denied that he had been leading an extravagant existence in London while his family were practically starving in Norfolk. This theme was explored further during Roland Oliver's cross-examination. He read out a letter written by Davidson in November 1931 to the Duchess of Devonshire. The letter, penned in purple ink, was of the begging variety (he had asked for a loan of £500, secured against a life insurance policy):

> I have my wife and four children still wholly dependent upon me at home practically without coal or food, as my credit has now been stopped by my local tradespeople until I can re-establish it by paying off about £80 due to the grocer, butcher, coal-merchant and baker. My bank has refused me a further overdraft and has in fact dishonoured the last three or four cheques I had drawn… I think I can say I have done many years of good work and it is terrible to be smashed up like this at the end of my life, especially before my children, who are really very talented, are started fairly in life.[3]

Roland Oliver began his cross-examination of Davidson with an immediate attack on his lack of morals. While his family lived in abject poverty in Stiffkey, asserted Oliver, the rector was cavorting around London with his girls, paying their rent and treating them to visits to restaurants and theatres. Davidson hotly denied that this was true; in fact, he said, he was so broke at the time he wrote to the Duchess that

2 The song comes from a comic opera of 1886 called *Dorothy*, written by B. C. Stephenson. The original production enjoyed modest success but was disastrously revived in 1908 by Davidson's notorious former schoolmate Maundy Gregory. Gregory even managed to convince Davidson to invest £200 in the production but it collapsed when the revenues from ticket sales began to disappear into his friend's pockets. The song's engaging refrain goes as follows:

> Why should we wait 'til tomorrow?
> You are Queen of My Heart tonight.

3 Letter from Harold Davidson to the Duchess of Devonshire dated 24 November 1931. Presented as Letter no. 72 in the court exhibits.

he had been forced to suspend his charitable work. Oliver questioned the rector in detail about his perilous financial state. Davidson admitted that he had been in dire financial straits since his 1925 bankruptcy, surviving on £420 a year. He flew into a rage when Oliver questioned him about Mr Gordon, particularly when an attempt was made to depict them as partners in crime:

> Oliver: Quite frankly, I am suggesting he is just a sort of swindler.
> Davidson: You will be able to judge that when you see him.
> Oliver: And that you have to some extent acted with him?
> Davidson: That is absolutely untrue. If you dare to say it outside the court I will deal with it.

Oliver asked him about some shares which Gordon had taken over from him and the rector again became incensed:

> Davidson: I am being charged with sexual immorality not financial immorality. If the Bishop of Norwich will frame another charge I will be delighted to meet it.
> Oliver: One of the things we have to test is as to whether you are a truthful person, and these questions are for that purpose.
> Davidson: You have just accused me of being a swindler. If you will frame another charge I shall be pleased to meet it.

Davidson turned to Chancellor North and asked if one of the charges could be amended to include a charge of fraud. This remark created pandemonium in the public gallery, where the motley audience included supporters of the rector, journalists, rubberneckers and even a contingent of homeless from the local Salvation Army Hostel. Many of them broke into spontaneous and prolonged applause at Davidson's show of defiance. The Chancellor ordered three uniformed policemen to clear the gallery.

For Harold Davidson Tuesday 24 May was another day spent under cross-examination. The day began with the rector discoursing at some length about Barbara's letter to the Bishop of Norwich. This letter was hugely important to the trial and was in fact the pivot on which the entire case revolved. Davidson's remarks reflect his belief that there was something decidedly suspect about the letter. He also discussed it in his pamphlet *The Reason Why*, written in 1934 long after the case was concluded. In his remarks in court he says that he was sure the letter was coached: 'it was not phrased in her way nor was it the expression of her mind.' What is surprising is that he does not blame the Bishop of Norwich's investigators for concocting the letter. Instead, he accuses the husband of Mrs Alice Lake, landlady at Providence Place, of persuading Barbara to involve herself in the case. Davidson thought it 'very likely that she consulted Mr Lake when they were writing the letter together, because the phraseology is so correct'. Oliver went on the offensive:

> Oliver: Are you not prepared to suggest anything whether it is the truth or not?
> Davidson: I am prepared to suggest any kind of dirty trick imaginable to this prosecution.

The blows continued to rain down on Davidson's reputation. Bishop Perrin, a lifelong friend of Davidson and head of the Actors' Church Union, was in court to hear Oliver ask the rector whether it was true that he had been expelled from the organisation in 1930 for falsely claiming to be its chaplain, and for being 'a little indiscreet'. Davidson half conceded that it was true but insisted that he was still a member and had simply agreed to change the title on his business card from 'Chaplain' to 'Priest-Associate'.

This was merely the warm-up for Oliver. He went on to ask about a girl called Lottie Green whom Davidson had helped in 1915. He had found her a job as a maid with a couple called Mrs and Mrs Price but it was not very long before they became suspicious of his motives and confronted him with the suggestion, in Oliver's words, that his 'relations with that young servant were not what they ought to be'. Davidson denied it and, while Oliver began to search among his papers for a letter that the rector had written to the Prices in March 1916, the depth of his anguish began to manifest itself:

> Davidson: I have been accused of misconduct with everyone I have been associated with for years. I have been misunderstood.
> Chancellor: Do you say misconduct? Do you mean in this case or generally?
> Davidson: No, I said misunderstood. I have been gossiped about by evil-minded people in connection with every young girl I have helped.

Chancellor: Before this case started?
Davidson: Oh yes, for years. I have been accused of being a white slave traffic agent, and that I took girls to my rooms and after prayer sold them to the Argentine. I was told that while this case was going on, and I was told that it was going to be proved in court.

Oliver produced the Price letter and quoted at length from it. Davidson had threatened to sue the Prices for slander if they made any further allegations about his relationship with Lottie Green. The verbal sparring between Oliver and Davidson continued all day. Oliver's strategy was to list a continuous sequence of events in which the rector's behaviour could be regarded as questionable, the idea being to build a gradual picture of the defendant as someone who was debased and immoral. Davidson countered each assertion by, in most cases, admitting that the incident had occurred but claiming that the only evil to be found was in the minds of his accusers. He referred to 'a lot of ridiculous gossip' and to 'evil-minded persons with minds like cesspools'. Oliver asked him if he were especially eager to 'meet girls between the age of sixteen and twenty' to which Davidson, with characteristic insouciance, replied: 'No. I like to get them from fourteen to twenty… The most impressionable ages in young girls who are going to be the mothers of the future generation are between fourteen to twenty and that is why I have always striven to get the highest principles inculcated into girls between those ages.'

The prosecution's strategy continued when Rose Ellis's name came up. They had already established that Rose Ellis was under Davidson's protection, had worked as his secretary and did a little sewing and bag-carrying from time to time. What was more difficult to prove, now that Rose had retracted her statement and would not be appearing as a witness, was that she was also the rector's mistress. The best they could come up with was that he had gone to her flat and had her dress a boil on his bottom. There followed one of the absurd, slightly surreal exchanges that had become the hallmark of this case. In the course of it Davidson famously denies that he has ever heard the word 'buttock':

Oliver: Is it your view of decency to go to a flat into which you went with a key and to get this pretty girl to dress your naked body?

Davidson: You are making the most outrageous suggestion. I have never said that.

Oliver: Was the boil on the buttock of your body? (Davidson does not immediately answer.) Have you to think?

Davidson: Yes, I do not know what the buttock is.

Oliver: Do you not know?

Davidson: Honestly I do not.

Oliver: Mr Davidson!

Davidson: It is a phrase honestly I have never heard. So far as I remember, it is a little below the waist.

Oliver: Are you serious?

Davidson: Honestly I have never heard it. When it was mentioned the other day I had to ask what it was.

Davidson went on to tell the court that he had taken Rose to a doctor to be treated for secondary syphilis (the most infectious phase of the disease). The Chancellor and the prosecutor, in keeping with the sensibilities of the time, were suitably horrified and this part of the trial is carefully omitted from the newspaper reports. Oliver asked Davidson how long Rose had suffered from it. His reply was that he didn't know and didn't really bother about it. His attitude to Barbara's bout of V.D. was the same; he helped her seek treatment but did not concern himself too much with the details; his implication being that since he did not have a sexual relationship with either woman, the state of their genitalia was of no concern to him. The prosecution thought otherwise. He had performed 'brothel duty' during his wartime service as a Navy chaplain, Oliver said, and he surely must been thoroughly well briefed about such diseases. Davidson replied that apart from his belief that '60 to 85 per cent of men' in the immediate postwar years were suffering from it, he actually knew very little.

If the prosecution made little progress on 24 May, they more than made up for it on the following day. Oliver attempted to show that Davidson and Mrs Betty Beach were conducting an affair. The rector admitted that he had stayed overnight at her house and had put his arm around her shoulder but emphatically denied that he had, as Barbara had claimed, embraced her while she was in her nightdress. It was also untrue, he said, that Betty had put on a gymnastic display for them in her nightdress and in true Davidson-style he began a little tap-dance in the witness-box – exclaiming that this was what Mrs Beach had performed. Most of Oliver's jabs missed the mark but when he began to produce photographs of the rector in compromising positions Davidson's credibility started to buckle under the strain. The first was a small, photo-booth image of the rector and Mrs Beach both dressed to the nines, with Davidson in a wing-collar and his companion elaborately coiffed and bejewelled. Davidson has a slightly demonic expression and rests his head against Mrs Beach's blonde locks, looking eerily like a vampire in a 1920s silent film. The photo of course was posed: Davidson said that, 'They were taken with a view of registering expressions for the cinema' and that he had 'shown them all to the Bishop of Norwich'. The problem for Davidson was that in this particular photograph he had a rather louche, proprietorial look. It did nothing to help dispel the accusations that confronted him.

Oliver asked him why he needed to be in any of the photographs at all, if they were simply intended to help his actress friends to develop their careers:

Davidson: It helps them to act. Suppose they are acting the part to my 'father', or to my 'lover'.
Oliver: Which does the photograph depict you as – the father or the lover?
Davidson: I should think the villain by the look of me. (Laughter.) It is a most horrible expression, the worst type of villain you could see.

Oliver's offensive continued. He recalled Barbara's evidence that Davidson had tried to rape her at the Alderney Street flat. Not only did the rector deny that he had made advances to her, he had said during his examination by the defence that it was Barbara who had assaulted him. Despite relentless pressure from Oliver, Davidson refused to budge from his story:

Oliver: That was a disgusting assault she made upon you if it is true?
Davidson: It was disgusting to me.
Oliver: I suggest it is the foulest lie?
Davidson: It is absolutely true. I doubt whether she did it from the point of view of corruption…

Oliver: She is only sixteen, twining her legs round you?
Davidson: Yes.
Oliver: Putting her tongue in your mouth?
Davidson: Very horrible. It nearly made me sick.
Oliver: Could you imagine a more abandoned little creature, if your evidence is true, or half of it?
Davidson: She was not abandoned, not in that way. She had some very remarkable qualities of character.

In the preface to Karilyn Collier's account of her grandfather's life, she makes the important point that a priest will never divulge information given to him in confidence, nor will he defend himself by condemning others. She says that the defence's strategy throughout the trial was to avoid all criticism of those who had impugned his name – including the bishop's investigators and the witnesses for the prosecution – and to rely on an appeal to overturn the verdict if he were to be found guilty. This does indeed ring true during the course of the trial: with the possible exception of Davidson's anger when the matter of his fifth child's parentage was raised it is difficult to find a single example of the rector speaking ill of anyone. It hardly applies, however, to Davidson's conduct while the case was still under investigation – he told Barbara's landlady that she had been in prison and, in a letter to the Bishop of Norwich, refers to Rose Ellis as 'mentally defective'. In both instances the intention appears to have been to undermine their credibility.

When Harold Davidson entered the witness-box on the morning of 25 May he still had a fighting chance to secure an acquittal but by mid afternoon he was sunk. After the lunchtime recess the prosecution delivered its two-stage *coup de grâce*. Roland Oliver produced a postcard-sized photograph in which the hapless rector stands gazing intently at the nubile, bare-shouldered form of fifteen-year-old Estelle Douglas. The photograph was the work of two unnamed Fleet Street photographers and the girl was the daughter of Mae Douglas, one of Davidson's closest friends. He had helped Mae to embark upon a stage career some twenty years before, and in an interview just before the trial began she had told the *Daily Herald* of her fondness for the rector and her belief in his innocence.

As Oliver questioned Davidson, the details of how the photograph was taken began to emerge. Mae Douglas had been eager to get Estelle into films and had asked Davidson to arrange a photo shoot to produce some publicity shots of the girl in a bathing suit. The initial plan was for it to be done at the Stiffkey rectory on Palm Sunday and the rector, Estelle, the photographer and three other girls had gone to stay for the weekend with this in mind. Some exceedingly ill-judged shots of the rector conducting a pyjama party at the rectory on the eve of his trial have survived. What could Davidson possibly have been thinking? Had he gone completely mad? The photos were pretty innocent but one is compelled to ask how a rational person, who had been charged with offences of immorality involving young women, could possibly have agreed to be photographed with a group of them drinking tea in their pyjamas? Worse was to come. The photographer did not have sufficient film to complete the shots of Estelle and a second photo-shoot was arranged for Easter Monday, at Estelle's mother's flat in Covent Garden, London.

On Easter Monday Estelle, Davidson, the same photographer and a colleague all met at Mae Douglas's flat. Mae was not present and, according to Davidson, the second photographer had immediately suggested that they get some saucy, semi-nude photos of Estelle posing with the rector. Davidson had immediately rejected the idea, he said, and on at least three occasions during his examination by Roland Oliver he claimed that Christopher Searle (the bishop's inquiry agent) had offered the men £125 to obtain an incriminating photo of him. Estelle gave evidence herself on 30 May and the details of what happened next are to be found in her testimony. She went to her room to change into a chemise and a bathing costume and came back to the sitting room wrapped in a black, tasselled Spanish shawl. One of the photographers told her that the strap of her bathing costume and her chemise were both showing and, apparently out of earshot of the rector, asked her to remove them. She came back into the room wearing just the shawl and stood with the rector while a series of photographs were taken.

Things looked bad enough for Davidson when Roland Oliver produced the first photograph but when the second photograph was presented the trial's defining moment arrived. It is virtually identical to the first photograph except that he is now in front of an aspidistra in a pot and Estelle's shawl has slipped, revealing her bare back, bottom and thighs. As stitch-ups go, the photograph is a masterpiece. The diminutive rector is looking straight into Estelle's eyes, with one hand on her shoulder and the other holding the shawl against her hip. It looks for all the world like the classic stereotype of the prurient, ageing parson seducing the young virginal innocent. Davidson's friend and press agent J. Rowland Sales told Tom Cullen that Davidson was poleaxed by the revelation that the photo existed: 'Davidson's face was a study when the prosecutor handed him this photograph for identification...The horrified disbelief written on it was not feigned...This was Davidson's moment of truth...'

While it is quite obvious that Davidson had no idea that Estelle was naked when the photograph was being taken, the clearest explanation of how it was obtained comes not from the rector but from the girl's own account and from an interview given by the rector's son to Tom Cullen. In her evidence on 30 May, Estelle told Richard Levy that as the flash went off the shawl 'was twitched or slipped'. Someone either pulled the shawl from behind or it fell from her shoulders, she said. There is no suggestion at all that Estelle colluded with the photographers; she testified that she had told her mother as soon as she realised that she had been photographed naked. An expert in photographic techniques, called as witness on 1 June, told the court that if the shawl had dropped just as the flash was exploding it would have left a shadow on the photograph (there was none). He does not, however, discount the possibility that it dropped a fraction of a second before.

There is more to the story of the photograph. Davidson later told his son that one of the photographers had offered him £50 to pose for a photo with Estelle Douglas, with the intention of selling it to the newspapers. Davidson was clearly tempted by the offer; he was broke and in desperate need of funds for his defence. His defence counsel contacted Nugent and told him 'not to let Father out of our sight for fear that he might do something foolish'. Nugent, his fiancée and the rector were in a café in Covent Garden on Easter Monday when Davidson excused himself for a few minutes to run an errand. Nugent waited and, when he failed to return, he and his fiancée rushed to Mae Douglas's flat in Endell Street, arriving just in time to see the flash of the camera.

It must be remembered that this case was tried without a jury. It would be Chancellor North who would decide Davidson's fate and, after the second photograph was produced, the portents were not good. North was wholly untutored in the ways of the world. His son Roger, a friend of Major Hamond's son Richard, assisted at the trial and at one stage had to kick his father under the table to prevent him from revealing that he had never heard of Greta Garbo. North was holding the second photograph when Davidson leaned towards him to remark upon some detail. The exchange that followed did not bode well for the rector:

Chancellor North: Keep your distance, sir. Don't explain it to me. You can explain it to Mr Oliver and see if you can make him believe it.

Ryder Richardson (to the Chancellor): I wish to draw your attention to the remark that has just fallen from your lips. Even in this matter I hope you will allow Mr Davidson to explain it to you, and not only to Mr Oliver....

Chancellor: I am trying to be as much like a machine as I can, but I am only human.

Richardson: I hope you will not only be human, but you will also be judicial...

The drama continued when the trial resumed on Thursday 26 May. By mid-afternoon Roland Oliver had completed his cross-examination of the rector and the strain was beginning to show. Davidson complained of feeling unwell and was allowed to stand down for a break before Ryder Richardson re-examined him. During the day Oliver had mounted a relentless assault on Davidson's character and judgement – the implication was that the rector was either debauched or he was a fool. Davidson believed that the flash had made him drop the shawl or that it had been pulled from his fingers. The record of his replies to Oliver's questions depicts a man drowning in details:

Oliver: If you were holding the drapery firmly you must have felt it leave your fingers?

Davidson: I didn't, it may have been the sudden flash that made me start.

Oliver: You said yesterday that the lady was to be photographed for the purpose of advertising a bathing costume. She is naked but for the shawl?

Davidson: That is the disgraceful part. I thought it was there....Until I saw it [the photograph] I had not the faintest idea the bathing costume was not on... You consider me guilty of having that photograph taken. What sensible man would have such a photograph taken the day before his trial? If I did I should be certified as insane at once.

It became clear that the two photographers had got the idea from the *Daily Herald* article in which Mae Douglas describes how she entrusted her daughter to Davidson's care. They had approached him and, he said, 'suggested a photograph which [he] considered utterly and entirely improper, although [he] was almost starving at the time'.

> Oliver: What sort of opinion of your character must 'B' and 'C' [the two photographers] have?
> Davidson: They said their opinion of my character was that it was so pure that no one in the world would think anything wrong of it. They said 'Why not have that photograph published so that the world will know the day before your case is taken and it will proclaim your innocence?' I said it would if the world thought as highly of me as they did, but it didn't... I was offered a very tempting sum of money, and I refused to have anything to do with it.

After the lunchtime adjournment the newspapers reported that 'hundreds of people' attempted to rush the doors of Church House to gain entry to watch the trial. In the mêlée that followed several women were trampled and the police had to force the doors shut to keep out the mob. The trial was already the subject of huge press attention but reports of the nude photographs produced during the previous day's proceedings raised the level of public interest in the trial to fever pitch.

It is significant that droves of female admirers came to watch the trial; the rector was obviously not without his charms. Davidson's cross-examination was cut short when he complained of feeling unwell. He was allowed to stand down and Mrs Jessie Walton, the rector's landlady at Macfarlane Road, Shepherd's Bush, was called instead. She flatly refuted any suggestion that anything had occurred between Davidson and Barbara. When Davidson was at home Barbara slept in her daughter's room and only ever occupied the rector's room when he was away at Stiffkey. The worst that could be said of the rector, Mrs Walton told the court, was that he kept very odd hours and hardly slept; lived on little but scrambled egg and tea and rushed around kissing everyone and addressing them as 'Queen of My Heart'. He even kissed her husband, she said. The rector was a man of 'large heart' who made a fuss of everyone about him whereas Barbara (for whom she clearly had little regard) spent her days in bed or sitting around reading novels or sketching.

The day's proceedings concluded with a brief reference to the ill-fated Nellie Churchill, now in a psychiatric hospital in Ewell, Surrey. The court would have to go to interview her there. Davidson, now a national celebrity, left the court to find the street filled with cheering crowds.

When the trial resumed the following day, 27 May, Mrs Walton was asked a few final questions before Davidson took the stand again. Roland Oliver concluded his cross-examination of the rector with more attacks on his probity. The night before the November 1931 Armistice Day commemorations, instead of being in Stiffkey preparing for the service, Davidson had said that he was confined to bed in Shepherd's Bush with a stomach upset. The prosecution claimed that he was, in reality, in bed with Barbara Harris and accused him of spending night after night with her in his room. In fact, he replied, he had entertained a different young woman in his room that evening: an eighteen-year-old aspiring actress called Gladys Clarke, who had spent her visit sewing on his medals. He added that it was perfectly possible to entertain a young woman in his room without being compromised: 'As a clergy-man one spends one's whole life in bedrooms.'[4]

Davidson's defence team went on to re-examine the rector. One of his lawyers, K. J. P. Barraclough, quoted at length from the furious letter Davidson had written to the Bishop of Norwich on 12 January 1932 (a section of the letter is cited on pages 34–5). In it Davidson rages against the bishop's 'hypocrisy' and 'duplicity'. It was also revealed that he had requested an interview with the Bishop of London on 20 Febru-ary, hoping to call him as witness for the defence, but the bishop had refused to see him.[5] It was also revealed that Davidson's wife had

4 The phrase '[a] life in bedrooms' is one of the most memorable of the entire trial and was the title of a 1960s play about the Davidson affair.
5 The Bishop of London was an old friend of Davidson and did, in fact, appear briefly for the defence on 31 May. He told the court that although the rector could be 'a very great nuisance' and that his financial affairs were a mess, he had never heard any suggestion of immoral behaviour made against him.

suffered two or three strokes brought on, he said, by the stress of the trial. He was desperate that she not be called to give evidence unless it was deemed to be vital to the proceedings.

On Saturday 28 May prosecution and defence continued with their respective endeavours to present the rector either as a serial adulterer or as a slightly dotty eccentric. Roland Oliver accused Mrs Walton of fabricating her evidence in order to protect the rector – an accusation she emphatically denied. John Beach, the husband of Betty Beach, the subject of the fourth charge, followed her onto the stand. Attempts by the prosecution to paint his wife as a 'scarlet woman' and to portray her as Davidson's lover foundered when Beach gave his replies to questions posed by the defence:

Levy: Is your wife of loose character?
John Beach: She is very much the opposite. I have never known a woman so modest.
Levy: Is the rector a welcome visitor?
Beach: Very welcome.
Levy: Would he be a welcome visitor if you thought he had designs on your wife?
Beach: I know he wouldn't. He is the last man in the world to have designs on my wife.

The defence followed John Beach with Mrs Walton's son, then with an anonymous young woman who lived in the next room at the Walton house, and finally with Mr Walton senior. All said that the rector was an extraordinary man who wandered about the house at all hours of the day and night, kissed everyone and anyone (including the milkman), and drank copious quantities of tea; but that he was not a lecher. When Oliver prodded Mr Walton senior, an Evangelist preacher, suggesting that he had perjured himself to shield the rector, he exploded: 'I am an older man than you and don't insult me. I have sworn nothing wrong.'

Mr Walton poured vitriol on Barbara's character. He described her as 'a liar from beginning to end', 'a bad, bad woman' and 'too bad to live'. 'Hell is not bad enough for a girl like that,' he said, to a faint ripple of applause in the back of the court.

When the trial resumed on Monday 30 May the court heard from Betty Beach. She and Davidson were no more than friends, she said, and nothing had ever occurred between them. Furthermore, she had seen nothing untoward occur between the rector and Barbara or any of the other women she had seen him help. Betty said that Barbara's evidence was plainly lies, and described Davidson as 'no ordinary man', whose behaviour was never anything but proper.

Estelle Douglas followed Betty onto the stand. Whatever the circumstances that had led to her posing nude with the rector, she said, he was not to blame. She had innocently agreed to the photo-shoot to further her ambition to become an actress.

On 1 June the case resumed in the Judges' Quadrangle at the Law Courts, displaced from Church House by an ecclesiastical convocation. There was more testimony about the photograph – a Mr Albert Darbyshire offered expert but inconclusive evidence that in his opinion the photo was either posed (that both Davidson and Estelle were willing parties to it), or that the shawl had been pulled away or dropped a fraction of a second before the flash. If the shawl had dropped *during* the flash the photograph would have appeared blurred.

Nugent Davidson, the rector's twenty-three-year-old son, took the stand and described the poverty in which the family lived. Credit had been stopped in November 1931 (the month that the rector had written his begging letter to the Duchess of Devonshire), and while they were not exactly starving there was no coal and very little food to be found at the rectory. Nugent described his father's charitable work, recalling one occasion in 1927 when they had both spent the night sitting in cafés and tramping the streets of London because his father had given his room to two girls who had walked to the capital from Edinburgh.

After Nugent came Lady Waechter, a friend of Davidson for twenty-four years. They had met, she said, during a shared association with the Dumb Friends' League – the old name for the animal welfare charity the Blue Cross. For twenty years Davidson had brought literally hundreds of girls, 'any conceivable kind of girl who was in any sort of trouble', to Evelyn Waechter's house. They were brought 'for money, clothes or work and sometimes for just a little friendship', she said, and she had always tried to provide help. A rare exception was Barbara Harris, whom Evelyn Waechter had met but considered to be beyond help. Ryder Richardson asked her to summarise Davidson's character and she replied that he was 'a very excellent man. A little eccentric, a little indiscreet, but of the highest moral standing in every possible way. I have never heard a word against him.'

On 2 June the case edged towards its conclusion with evidence taken in chambers from Nellie Churchill, still a patient at the mental hospital in Ewell and the last witness in this protracted, complex case. Richard Levy announced that he would not be calling Davidson's associate, the nefarious Arthur Gordon, ostensibly because he had nothing 'vital or really relevant' to offer to the case but also, presumably, because of a fear that the rector would suffer guilt by association from his appearance in court. The prosecution then dropped several parts of the charges against Davidson: specifically the accusations relating to Betty Beach, to a Miss Williams, to Violet Lowe (the waitress in the Bloomsbury Chinese restaurant) and to several women Davidson is alleged to have approached in various hotel lobbies and on the London Underground.

In Nellie Churchill's written testimony she said that Davidson had never made an improper suggestion to her. When they were found in the dark together, she said, they really were trying to relight the gas. After lunch Richard Levy began his summing up for the defence. He made a strong, impassioned plea for the rector to be acquitted. Davidson, said Levy, was an 'unusual and eccentric' man but one who, when asked by the court, had insisted that he be judged by ordinary standards of behaviour. Levy said that 'one might as well ask a lunatic if he were sane'. The rector followed his own conscience and was oblivious to the possible consequences:

> You have seen that he is a man completely and utterly indifferent to the way other people judge his behaviour. He has been engaged on work upon which he has set his heart, which has involved conduct in which most people would not be involved, and he does not realise that his conduct has left him open to misunderstanding and misrepresentation...

Levy continued his closing speech on the following day, Friday 3 June, and among the crowds that packed the courtroom was Rose Ellis. It was revealed that the trial had already cost the prosecution £6,000 with the cost of shorthand recording alone running to £1,000. As a comparison, a typical vicar's salary at the time was about £400 per annum. Over one million words of testimony had been transcribed and the financial strain placed upon Harold Davidson had been severe; he had already spent more than £1,500 on his defence. Levy spoke of the Estelle Douglas photograph, questioning the prosecution's description of the image as that of a 'naked woman'. In fact, declared Oliver somewhat disingenuously, 'there is no more showing in that picture than you would see in women dancing in an hotel or on the cover of an art magazine.' It would have been a simple matter for the prosecution to call the two photographers to refute Davidson and Estelle's claims that they had no idea it was being taken but this, said Levy, they chose not to do. The prosecution did not call them because they knew perfectly well that it was an accident, he said.

Coming to the subject of Barbara Harris, Levy said that of all the hundreds of girls who had been associated with Davidson, she was the only one who had come before the court to claim that he had behaved improperly towards her. 'Perfectly respectable people against whom there can be no word' had come forward to contradict her evidence, declared Levy, 'You are asked to ruin this man's career and his life for all time on the uncorroborated evidence of that girl.' 'That girl', he said, 'lay in bed during the day, went to cafés in the evening, and slept with men all night.' He launched a coruscating attack on the prosecution for making payments to Barbara; an inducement, he said, for her to continue her debauched existence:

> She has been taken under the wing of the prosecution, given board and lodgings, and pocket money so that she could continue the sort of life that she had been living. Yet according to her sister, while living at the expense of the prosecution, she has still been going about with men, and still selling her body on the streets of London... The way this girl has been treated seems almost to put a premium on vice.

Barbara's accusations against the rector were actuated by spite, declared Levy. The cause, he suggested, might have been Barbara's visit to the Stiffkey rectory in July 1931, which ended when she and Rose hitchhiked their way back to London and slept in fields along the way. Alternatively, he proposed, Davidson might have infuriated her by refusing to respond to her sexual advances, or perhaps her dissolute life had left her mentally unbalanced. His address lasted for three and a half hours and it ended with a passionate plea directed, of course, to the one person who would be deciding the outcome of the case – the Chancellor:

> I ask you to stand between this man and persecution. You will be
> the means of putting an end finally, and completely to a career,
> whatever you may think of its peculiarities and eccentricities, that
> has been useful to society. You have to say that this man shall be
> damned and ruined and that his family shall never again look
> people in the face.
>
> If you prefer the voice of scandal and suspicion to the voice of
> tolerance and understanding, if you prefer evidence from sources
> that are tainted with vice and falsehood to the evidence of people
> who are decent, and honest, and virtuous, if you prefer the
> assumption of guilt to the assumption of innocence, to which
> every man is entitled, then and then only will you find that these
> charges are proved.
>
> If you do, I say that this case will leave an indelible stain on the
> fair name of justice in this country, and will reflect lasting discredit
> upon those responsible for such a prosecution.

Roland Oliver countered with a closing speech that spanned three days and lasted for a total of fourteen hours. He lambasted the notion that the photographs taken of Estelle were insignificant to the case. On the contrary, declared Oliver, they 'threw a flood of light on the whole matter'. He described the photographs as 'infamous' and said that they were taken for only one purpose: 'to sell as the notorious rector of Stiffkey with one of his girls, in foreign countries.' The real reason that he had not called the two photographers as witnesses was that they were 'cynical and wicked' men who were in cahoots with the rector. The rector was 'an awful liar' whose statements to the court were a 'labyrinth of lies'.

In contrast, he told the court, Barbara should be regarded as 'one of the most truthful witnesses you have ever heard'. The depth and breadth of the rector's alleged duplicity were explored when Oliver resumed his closing speech on 4 June. Oliver cited thirty-nine separate instances when Davidson had, he claimed, contradicted himself in the witness-box. Among them was the rector's statement that he had told Mrs Walton that Barbara had been afflicted with V.D. Mrs Walton had denied knowing it and would have thrown her out if she had, she had said. The implication was that Davidson's claim that he could not possibly have been sexually interested in Barbara because of her condition was a blatant lie; she had only believed that she had it and the rector knew this. Another lie was the rector's assertion that he 'knew nothing' of the whereabouts of the negatives of the Estelle Douglas photographs. During his re-examination he had completely contradicted his original statement, saying that he had seen the negatives handed over to the two photographers.

Oliver went on to question why two of the principal players in the drama, Davidson's wife Molly and Rose Ellis, had not been called by the defence. Excuses had been offered for the non-appearance of both women but the real reason that they had not been called, he contended, was that they might expose Harold Davidson for the liar that he was. Davidson had persuaded Rose to retract her statement, asserted Oliver, but the rector could not risk Rose breaking down in the witness-box and telling the truth about their affair. In Mrs Davidson's case, declared Oliver, the defence had claimed that she had been too ill to appear but what they actually feared was that she would let slip her true feelings about the rector's girls.

Oliver had been speaking for eight and a half hours when his voice began to fail him. Chancellor North granted an adjournment until Monday 6 June when Oliver would conclude his speech. 6 June was, in fact, the twenty-fifth and final day of the trial; 'one of the longest and most notorious trials for a long time,' commented Chancellor North during that day's opening remarks. A packed courtroom heard Roland Oliver conclude his closing speech, with both Harold Davidson and Barbara Harris there to hear it. Barbara, he said, had been vilified throughout the case as lazy, deceitful and little more than a prostitute. Oliver contended that she was none of these things:

> I wonder how many people in this court have been abandoned at the age of fifteen, left without a home or a roof over [their] head, with a mother in an asylum, a father dead, and a brother who would not have anything to do with her, and a sister in domestic service and incapable of helping. I should think that a girl of fifteen in such a situation would have called for a little sympathy.
>
> One thing flung at Barbara continuously from the beginning to the end of this case is that she is a prostitute. I suggest that it is

perfectly obvious that Barbara has never been that. When we first hear of her in Miss Bevan's house, here is this girl, an exceedingly pretty girl, practically starving, unable to pay the 10 shillings a week rent, and trying to get a little money by doing little jobs and needlework. There were no coals, and therefore she stopped in bed because it was too cold to get up. These facts surely prove that she was not a prostitute...

Despite attempts by the defence to undermine her credibility, Oliver said that Barbara 'had a wonderful memory and was a very truthful girl'. Davidson's remarks about Barbara during the trial were 'a disgraceful, blackguardly picture of the girl's character... an abominable series of inventions for the purpose of damning her for the rest of her life...' Barbara went back to the rector time after time because he was a last resort; he represented a roof and food for someone on the brink of being driven out onto the streets.

If Barbara had made up the whole story, declared Oliver, surely she would have claimed that their relationship had been a sexual one. No one would have been able to disprove it if she had, he said, but she had consistently denied that any of the rector's attempts to seduce her had succeeded. It had also been suggested that she craved the limelight. If this was her intention she had certainly succeeded, but Oliver also drew the court's attention to a line in her letter to the Bishop of Norwich in which she pleads for her name to be kept out of the affair because of her family and her landlady. He went on to pour scorn on the suggestion that she had been bribed to implicate the rector: when she wrote her letter, he claimed, 'she had been seen by no one and had not received a penny'.

Oliver dismissed the evidence of the Waltons, who loved Davidson and loathed Barbara in more or less equal measure, as nothing less than perjury: 'The whole population of the [Walton] house were apparently in and out of his room at all hours of the night for the purpose of showing that Barbara was not there. It is a very badly constructed series of lies. They have gone too far in their desire to get the bedroom so heavily populated that Barbara could not have hidden anywhere.'

Oliver described Davidson as the worst kind of hypocrite. He introduced Barbara to Mrs Lake (her new landlady) as a 'thoroughly respectable little girl' and yet, when the bishop's investigators began to circle, he mounted a relentless campaign to discredit her both to the Lakes and in the press. Since the beginning of February Davidson had conducted 'an infamous press campaign', said Oliver. Richard Levy had asserted during his closing remarks that any conviction would 'leave an indelible stain on the fair name of justice in this country'. This statement, said Oliver, 'was obviously addressed not to you [Chancellor North] but to the public, and was intended to be an invitation or an incitation to the public to think that the case had never been properly proved or that you had been influenced by prejudice and had not acted fairly upon the evidence.'

With Oliver's speech finally concluded, the court was adjourned until 10.30 am on Friday 8 July when Chancellor North would deliver his verdict. As Davidson left the court, surrounded by his friends and supporters, he told a journalist that he would go back to Stiffkey to wait for the verdict, 'praying that the truth may prevail'. He had given an undertaking not to preach while he waited for the verdict but told the same reporter that he 'felt at perfect liberty to do so' if he wished.

6

Verdict

Any hopes the Church may have had that Harold Davidson would keep a low profile until the verdict was announced were quickly dispelled on the following Sunday, 12 June. By now the rector was a major celebrity and the press reported everything he did, and almost everything that he said. The headlines in the *Eastern Daily Press* of 13 June were typical and refer to the dramas of the previous day:

SCENES IN STIFFKEY CHURCH

REV. H. DAVIDSON'S UNEXPECTED RETURN

OTHER CLERGY WHO WERE ASKED TO PREACH

A PROTEST AT THE LECTERN

By late evening on Saturday 11 June Davidson had still not returned to Stiffkey and H. S. Radcliffe, the Archdeacon of Lynn, had consequently arranged for two neighbouring clergymen to take the Sunday services. With minutes to go before the morning service there were about sixty people in church, including several reporters, and the police were on hand to maintain order and direct traffic. The Revd W. Harcourt of Wighton had been deputed to take over but as he stepped forward to begin Davidson swept into the church, accompanied by an Irish-Liverpudlian nurse in an orange hat whom he introduced as his secretary. Harcourt immediately ceded the lectern and left the church and Davidson took the service, taking for his theme that 'The wages of sin are death, but the gift of God is eternal life'. There was a telegram from Archdeacon Radcliffe waiting for Davidson at the church stating that he had been unable to contact him and had consequently 'provided for the services at Stiffkey and Morston until the case has ended'. Davidson told a reporter that he had consulted his solicitors and 'decided to resume full duties' at Stiffkey and Morston. The Archdeacon of Lynn was interviewed in time for the Monday papers and was asked for a reaction to Davidson's statement: 'If he wishes to carry on now, I believe he can, but is it wise? I think it would be wiser for him not to preach until the case is concluded – wiser from his own point of view and wiser for the Church. Can it do him or the Church any good at the moment?'[1]

In the afternoon Davidson preached at Morston church, the service passing off without incident, but soon after it ended a large crowd began to gather on the green in front of Stiffkey church. The throng of several hundred included most of the village, numerous day-trippers and the same contingent of police that had been at the morning service. As the bell began to toll for evensong the Revd R. H. Cattell, the rector of Warham, arrived to take the service. Cattell, a former captain of the England rugby team with seven daughters, told one of the reporters present that he was acting on orders from the Bishop of Norwich and would still take the service even if Davidson showed up.

There were 200 people in church as the service got under way but Cattell barely had time to open his prayer book when the rector's car pulled up. The service continued for some time while notes were passed and whispered exchanges took place between the two vicars and the parish clerk.[2] Davidson then approached the lectern just as one of the psalms was coming to an end and grabbed the Bible that Cattell was using. For some moments the two men wrestled for control of the Bible until finally Cattell gave up and stood aside, mopping his brow with a handkerchief. As Davidson, in a trembling voice, read the second lesson Cattell sent off one of his parishioners to summon the policemen who were on crowd control duty outside but they declined to intervene. As

1 Quoted in the *Eastern Daily Press*, 13 June 1932.
2 Cattell provided more details about the incident to a reporter during the following week. He said that the note Davidson had passed him was written in purple ink and stated, 'I have arranged to take over duty with approval of the Bishop's solicitors and my own. The Archdeacon has been informed and I understand agreed. There will be a grave scandal if you attempt to prevent my preaching.' Quoted in the *Eastern Daily Press*, 20 June 1932.

soon as the lesson ended Cattell stood up in front of the congregation
and exclaimed:

> I am extremely sorry this has happened. It reduces the service to a
> farce. I have received my orders from my superior officer, the
> Bishop, to take this service and no one else was to take it. As
> comparatively nothing short of force would prevent Mr Davidson
> taking part, I can see nothing left to do but to withdraw as I
> cannot conscientiously take part in a service in association with
> him. If Mr Davidson persists I will retire.[3]

A dozen or so members of the congregation walked out of the church
at this point, presumably in protest at Davidson's behaviour, but others
quickly came in to replace them. For several minutes there was pandemonium in the church as a group of women shouted and applauded.
The uproar did not finally subside until Davidson, standing beside the
altar, shouted 'Please, please, remember this is the House of God.'
Cattell quickly disrobed in the vestry and left, declaring to a news-
paperman that he would be reporting to the Bishop of Norwich. Davidson continued with the service, taking as his text the words 'Blessed are
the pure in heart for they shall see God'. At the end he shook hands
with many of his parishioners as they filed out, although the *Eastern
Daily Press* reporter did note that a few walked straight passed him.

In Archdeacon Radcliffe's interview with the press on 13 June he had
gone on to deplore the media circus that had enveloped Davidson's
parish. Many of the people attending the churches at Stiffkey and
Morston were there merely as sightseers, he said, and he hoped that
'something may be done to bring back the full spirit of worship to the
services'. It did seem, however, that no further attempts would be made
to prevent Davidson from holding services, at least until the verdict was
announced.

On the following Sunday, 19 June, the morning and evening services
were both packed; a reporter from the *Eastern Daily Press* noting that
people had begun arriving early in the morning, many bringing picnic
hampers with them. By evensong the crowd was so large that it over-
flowed into the churchyard. People stood on tombstones to catch a
glimpse of the rector and shake his hand and there was almost a party

3 Quoted in the *Eastern Daily Press*, 13 June 1932.

atmosphere inside the church – the reporter noted 'a sun-tanned girl in plus fours and youths with open-necked shirts' who had cycled or hiked to the village to see the great man. Davidson told a reporter that he had been inundated with offers to speak at theatres and lecture halls, including one proposal to tour America.

A week later Davidson was out and about in his parish once again, his every move scrutinised and reported by the ranks of journalists who were covering the story. The *Eastern Daily Press*, as ever, was at the vanguard of the press coverage. The Monday 27 June edition describes the rector's movements on the previous day and contains numerous clues as to his state of mind and to the manner in which the local community had become divided by the issue. The paper reported that Davidson took a morning service at Morston, where he prefaced his sermon with the news that the Bishop of Norwich had written to him enclosing a letter sent to the Archdeacon of Lynn that, in the rector's view, entirely vindicated his actions at Stiffkey church a fortnight before.

As far as Davidson was concerned the matter was now closed. The congregation of about forty contained, the paper said, 'mainly visitors', a local girl played the harmonium, and a cloud of bees, swarming outside the only entrance, delayed the rector's departure at the end of the service. He eventually gave the bees and the *paparazzi* the slip and cycled along the coast road to Stiffkey, waving to day-trippers on a passing motor-coach. At Stiffkey church there was a crowd waiting for him as he arrived to conduct baptisms for three local children. Afterwards he posed for photographs and paused to sign autographs for yet more gawpers. In a prayer book proffered by one, he wrote what I believe was his personal credo: 'We are all in the gutter but some of us are looking at the stars.'[4]

By evensong people had come from far and wide and the roadside was lined with cars for a quarter of a mile. The rector was well qualified to expound on the subject chosen for his sermon – 'If kind things could not be said about people, it was kinder not to speak of them at all. It was possible to devastate a person's life by idle gossip.'

As he left the service the rector shook hands with the crowd and told a reporter that he was considering various offers of public engagements, including an offer from a Birmingham skating rink to perform

4 The quotation is from Oscar Wilde's play *Lady Windermere's Fan*.

his old vaudeville routine before 6,000 people. There was also a proposal, he said, for him to appear at a West End theatre and another offer of a part in a play. He was pondering all of these opportunities, he declared, but what must really have been occupying his thoughts during those final days of June was the forthcoming verdict.

The court reconvened at Church House, Westminster at 10.30 am on Friday 8 July. Two of the rector's children, Patricia and Nugent, were in court to hear Chancellor North's findings but the rector, true to form, was late. Davidson was formally acquitted of those parts of the charges relating to Betty Beach, to a Miss Williams, to Violet Lowe (the waitress in the Bloomsbury Chinese restaurant), and to several women Davidson is alleged to have importuned in various hotel lobbies and on the London Underground. North went on to deal with the remaining elements of the case against Davidson in detail. Davidson, he said, was not being tried for neglecting his parish or for financial irregularities, or even for his involvement in the photographs of Estelle Douglas: '...for all I have heard here he may be an exemplary parish priest. I am not trying him for any offence against the bankruptcy laws, obtaining money by false pretences, for conspiracy, perjury, subornation of perjury, or even the outrage on that child of fifteen, committed on the 28th of last March, at which he admits he was present.'[5]

North said that he had read and re-read every one of the 2,300 pages of shorthand notes taken during the trial. He had been as fair-minded as it was humanly possible to be, he declared, and the conclusions he had come to were his and his alone. Working through the charges in order he began with the allegation relating to Rose Ellis. The only thing that was in dispute, he said, was whether or not they had had a sexual relationship; it was undoubtedly true that their association had lasted for more than eleven years and that Davidson had shown her great kindness on many occasions. The problem was that he simply did not believe that she had ever been his secretary and the landladies who had been called spoke of incidents that left them suspicious and angry. In his view, North said, their suspicions were well founded: Davidson was keeping Rose Ellis, he had a key to her room and had been discovered there at 6 am He had also, by his own admission, taken her on two or

5 Norfolk Record Office, transcript of Chancellor North's judgment, July 1932.

three trips to Paris and stayed in the same hotel. This was all circum-
stantial but what really condemned the rector in Chancellor North's
eyes was his performance in the witness-box. Davidson, he said, was
'an awful liar':

> I watched him anxiously and carefully in the witness-box for
> something like four days. I do not believe him. His evidence in
> chief, even in the skilful and firm hands of Mr Richardson, was a
> tissue of absurdities, and Mr Oliver in cross-examination demon-
> strated it to be a mass of reckless and often deliberate falsehoods.
> He went down as an absolutely discredited witness on whose oath
> no reliance can be placed, nor do I think that such evidence as he
> has called has helped him in the least.[6]

North said that even if the prosecution's evidence had left him in any
doubt of the rector's guilt, 'his refusal to call three witnesses vital to
disprove the case against him would have clinched the matter'. If
Davidson was as innocent as he claimed, Arthur Gordon, Mrs Davidson and (above all) Rose Ellis should all have been immensely useful to
the defence's case. Rose Ellis in particular, who had retracted her allegations against the rector and publicly defended him, was in court
throughout the trial but had not been called by the defence. The rector,
he concluded, was guilty of this charge. This is an odd conclusion. A
basic tenet of British law is that the burden of proof is with the prosecution, not the defence. Yet Davidson is convicted on the first charge in
part because he fails to call witnesses to prove his innocence.

The Chancellor went on to deal with the second charge: that Davidson had made improper suggestions to Dorothy Burn, a waitress at the
Lyons café in Walbrook, London. Miss Burn, declared the Chancellor,
was a perfectly respectable girl who lived with her parents, had a
proper job and 'was in no need of being rescued, protected or helped'.
Her evidence, he said, was 'unassailable'. Davidson had pursued her
relentlessly – inviting her to tea, suggesting that she telephone him, flat-
tering her looks and following her into the staff cloakroom. This was
compounded by all of his talk of the evils of childless marriages, and
taken as a whole there was no doubt that the rector was guilty of
making the 'improper suggestions' referred to in the second charge: 'A

6 *ibid.*

virtuous woman has an instinct for diagnosing when a man is a wrong'un, and what his intentions are... I am compelled to find the defendant guilty...'

The Chancellor had already found Davidson guilty of two of the five charges when the rector entered the Great Hall and took his seat beside Richard Levy. He wore black clerical garb and carried a silk top hat and, according to his friend J. Rowland Sales, he sat for much of the time with his eyes fixed on the ceiling as if he were somewhere else. The Chancellor spent little time expounding on the third charge – that Davidson had committed an immoral act by embracing Barbara Harris in the Yeng Wah Restaurant in Bloomsbury – before convicting him of that too. The waitress who saw him do it was credible, said North, and even the rector had admitted that he might have put his arm around Barbara's shoulders.

The fourth charge – that Davidson had habitually associated himself with women of a loose character – was dealt with next. This charge related to Barbara Harris, to Mrs Betty Beach, to Miss Taylor and to other women whose names were not known. Mrs Beach's name had been dropped from the proceedings although this did not prevent North from giving a stern warning to her husband that he should keep a closer eye on her in the future. Mrs Beach, he said, should be more aware of 'the danger of lovely woman stooping to folly and flouting the rules of propriety and decency'.

And what of Barbara Harris's credibility? She, after all, was the well-spring of the evidence against Davidson; Rose Ellis had retracted hers and there was little in the testimony of other witnesses beyond vague accusations of 'pestering'. The basic facts were not in dispute: she and the rector had begun their relationship when she was sixteen and a half and it had continued for eighteen months. They had shared a room on many occasions and a bed too, if Barbara was to be believed. Chancellor North had already dismissed the rector as a liar and he had observed Barbara closely over three days of examination, cross-examination and re-examination. In his view she was a truthful witness:

.... if Barbara is not speaking the truth there is an end of this part of the case; so there is if Barbara's story is not corroborated... I have come to a definite conclusion. I believe Barbara. Is she corroborated? In my judgement she is. In my judgement it is important to observe that though she frankly admitted the bestowal of her favours on a number of men of all sorts, her story is that the defendant, although he fed, housed, and provided her with money and clothes, even a gold watch, and got her places from time to time, never succeeded in repeated attempts to enjoy them... If she was the wicked little liar Mr Levy would make me believe, I fail to see why she should stop short at attempts, and not try to fasten on the defendant the full guilt of completed adultery.[7]

He was satisfied that Davidson had made repeated attempts to frighten Barbara out of testifying; it would mean six months in prison for him, the rector had declared. North believed that Davidson's strategy had backfired; it had actually provoked her into writing her letter of complaint to the Bishop of Norwich. He found Davidson guilty of this, the fourth charge, both with regard to Barbara and to Miss Taylor.

The wronged ladies of the fifth and final charge were the waitresses at the ABC restaurant in Oxford Street, much pestered by the rector and whose teeth he was wont to admire; and poor Nellie Churchill, sometime artist's model and now confined in a Ewell asylum. Davidson had pulled back the lips of one girl like a horse to admire her teeth; behaviour that forced the Chancellor to conclude that the rector was 'mad'. It did not absolve him from the consequences, however, and of this charge too he was pronounced guilty.

North concluded the proceedings with the statement that he would refer the case to the Bishop of Norwich for sentencing, the actual date to be fixed by the bishop after the period allowed for appeal had elapsed. To add to Davidson's misery, Chancellor North awarded costs against him. The trial had cost the Church Commissioners more than £8,000 and given that his legal fees had already reduced Davidson to penury, North must have known that there was little prospect that these funds could be recovered. The newspapers of the time reported that as the court usher stood up to announce the adjournment of the proceedings, Harold Davidson snatched up his silk hat and sprinted the length of the aisle to the exit of the Great Hall. He found Richard Levy already standing in the lobby and grasped his hand, thanking him for

7 *ibid.*

all he had done. A group of supporters, including some clergymen, rushed forward to commiserate and to shake his hand and the newspapers reported, somewhat mischievously perhaps, that a young girl dashed forward to kiss him. Davidson noticed Rose Ellis standing beside the main staircase and shook her hand as well, before emerging from the building to join the crowds waiting outside.

MOLLY DAVIDSON

Throughout the long difficult days of 1932 Harold Davidson's wife kept out of the public eye. Her remarks at the family meeting that immediately preceded the trial were recorded and show that she was fiercely loyal to her husband and had not the slightest doubt that he was entirely innocent. It is therefore surprising, as Chancellor North observed, that she was not called as a witness for the defence. At the very least she would have been able to support the rector's contention that the visits to the Stiffkey vicarage of what she referred to as his 'stray cats' were for completely innocent reasons. Molly had suffered illness throughout much of 1932, including several small strokes brought on, according to Davidson, by the stress of the trial. Nevertheless, statements had been taken from the ailing Mrs Lake and the demented Nellie Churchill and read out in court, and it is therefore puzzling that the same was not done with Molly in spite of her illness. The only clues as to what she really thought of her husband and the accusations made against him are contained in a solitary interview, granted to the *Sunday Dispatch* newspaper on 10 July 1932, two days after his conviction.

Molly and her third child, Patricia, were asked for their views on the case. In the six months that had elapsed since the family meeting, Molly's loyalty to her husband had held fast but it was not unconditional; doubts had emerged about his judgement and his obduracy. An undercurrent of both bitterness and weariness can be detected in her remarks. Her man, it seems, had developed feet of clay:

> I will wager that not one of the many thousands he knows will say they ever heard Mr Davidson admit that he was wrong, or even that he has made a mistake...
>
> It is useless to tell a lunatic who says he is a poached egg, that

he is not one. It is vain to argue with him; he will exhaust your logic and outstrip your reasoning powers…

Mr Davidson is a very clever man who has made but poor use of the keen brain he possesses… People – perhaps because they are less limited than I – take off their hats to him. They say to me with bated breath: 'What a clever man your husband is' and I mentally register: 'What fools you are…'

Time and time again I have remonstrated with such arguments as this: no man can associate with one swindler (though that perhaps is a hard word to use, for one of these men whose ideas did not coincide with mine was a charming young man to meet[8] – let us say instead, wily charmer) after another, varying the association with that of the vilest dregs of humanity, without getting tarmarked. Such association is bound to have its evil effect sooner or later…

By the very forcefulness of his pleadings he has induced myself and two friends to take into our homes the refuse of humanity, because he hopes to make Magdalenes of all. He has pirouetted through life on a single text, 'Thank God I am not like the rest of men', and most devout is my reply – for the world's sake – 'Thank God you're unique.' Mr Davidson believes in himself. He will go on pirouetting, nor will this case or any other force him to deviate one tittle from the path he has chosen. I have tried for six or seven exhausting years to make him see my point of view. I have failed, and I am no mean opponent…

What will this case effect? Nothing. Who pays the piper? I do, and my children…

He has not been proved guilty, despite the verdict, so far as I am concerned. He will go on spending his money – money which, in my opinion, should have been spent at home – helping worthless characters, as he did before the case and since. In fact he will go on pirouetting exactly the same…

Is Mr Davidson a saint whom the powers of good protect, or does the Devil look after his own?[9]

8 Presumably Arthur John Gordon.
9 Mrs Molly Davidson in extracts from an interview with the *Sunday Dispatch* newspaper, 10 July 1932.

His daughter Patricia, who sets out her views in the same article, was similarly not blind to her father's faults. If anything, her verdict on her father's conduct was even harsher. The following are extracts from her remarks:

> It is...stupid...and a waste of time to try to help a man out of his little mud-hole when he openly shows you that he much prefers to caper about inside it, and does not really mind very much if he sticks there altogether...
>
> My father has made one eternal cry throughout his life. 'No one understands me.' I hope he is ready to admit that his is certainly a very difficult character to understand... He does the most extra-ordinary things at the oddest moment. He demands advice apparently for the sole purpose of acting in the contrary way, for he rarely acts on advice given, and when he is landed firmly 'in the soup' he meets all remonstrance with a battery of excuses, exhausting to the listener who for the sake of peace gives up the argument and leaves him triumphant. I need hardly say that he invariably emerges from a trying situation smiling and apparently none the worse off. He is, if one may use the phrase, a sort of human India-rubber ball rebounding with appalling persistence. It is in this capacity that he has succeeded in annoying more people in the last ten years or so than any ordinary man would in a lifetime...
>
> It is the fact that my father's thoughts do not in the least tally with his actions that is the cause of a good deal of his troubles throughout his life, and certainly it must account for his perpetual grievance of being misunderstood...
>
> His whole life, as far as I know it or have heard of it, has been one large eccentricity. He has always tried to do what other men would not or dared not do...
>
> He is impulsive. He does whatever pleases him at the moment, without thought of the future, regardless of outside opinion...[10]

Within a matter of a couple of days Harold Davidson had been stripped of his reputation, saddled with enormous court costs, criticised

10 Patricia (Paddy) Davidson, quoted in the same *Sunday Dispatch* article of 10 July 1932.

by his own family in the national press and made a public laughing stock. Whether the 'India-rubber ball', as Paddy called him, would be able to bounce back from these calamities would prove to be the ultimate test of his character.

7

Hell Hath No Fury Like a Parson Scorned

The day the *Sunday Dispatch* interview with his wife and daughter appeared, Harold Davidson was in hot water once again. Incredibly, given that he had been convicted on five separate counts of immoral behaviour, no decision had been taken by the Bishop of Norwich to bar him from preaching. Some of his parishioners had other ideas, however. When he arrived at Morston church to take the afternoon service he found the doors locked and the following notice written on a piece of cardboard:

> NOTICE
>
> This church was locked on Sunday 10th July as a public protest against the action of the Ecclesiastical authorities in allowing Mr Davidson to continue to take services here after his conviction. (Signed) PHILIP HAMOND, Acting Churchwarden.

Davidson prised the notice off with his penknife and, gathering the small congregation about him, sent a young girl into the village for a Bible and prayer book and then calmly conducted the service on the unmown churchyard grass. Philip Hamond, Davidson's bitter enemy, was not alone in his belief that an inhibition should have been applied against the rector at the trial's end. The case had in fact caused fault lines to develop in the parish. In simple terms, most of his parishioners loved him unconditionally but the local Norfolk Establishment hated him with a passion. His two most implacable adversaries were Hamond and Colonel Groom, a friend of the Major Hamond, who lived at Warborough House in Stiffkey. Davidson appears to have fallen out with Colonel Groom around 1912, when he rebuked him for discarding his wife and taking on a mistress.

The schism that developed also appears to have varied between the two churches within his parish: he seems to have aroused greater antipathy among the residents of Morston (perhaps as a result of Major Hamond's influence) than in Stiffkey. If the newspaper reports can be believed, this day, 10 July, was typical. Before arriving at Morston to find the church locked Davidson had conducted a morning service at Stiffkey before a friendly congregation of a hundred people. At the beginning of his sermon he made a passionate speech calling for the Consistory Court system to be reformed. He went on to say that Christ, too, had scandalised the religious leaders of the time, 'He consorted with the lowest of the low, both men and women, and particularly was He tender to women of the outcast class.'

As he left the church at the conclusion of the service the good people of Stiffkey crowded about him and an elderly parishioner handed him a box of cigars. On the notice board of the church was pinned a telegram, purportedly from a Dulwich church worker. It was addressed to the Churchwarden, Stiffkey and read: 'Stand by your rector. Don't be a Judas. God will reward you.'

The evening service was also at Stiffkey and afterwards Davidson invited the congregation to come over to the rectory, where he would address them on the lawn. He went into the rectory and discarded his clerical garb before coming out to talk about his trial to the villagers who milled about in the summer sunshine. He criticised the machinations of the Consistory Court – such cases should be tried in a court of law before a proper judge, he said. He thanked the village for supporting him through the trial and read a letter from a woman whom he'd helped a decade earlier. The author of the letter had been saved, she said, from 'I know not what' and was now happily married – all thanks to the efforts of Harold Davidson. The villagers gave him a rousing cheer as he spoke his final words: he would appeal the verdict to the Privy Council if he could raise the funds. He had told a reporter the night before that he intended to work to this end by returning to his old vocation – he was booked for the following week to perform a variety act at the Prince's Cinema, Wimbledon. As his flock filed slowly out of the rectory garden through its small wicket gate there was an air of defiance about Davidson as he shook their hands.

The beleaguered pastor drew some comfort, at least, from what by the standards of the day was an incendiary article in the following Friday's *Church Times*. In a front page article the powerful and influential paper directed criticism at almost everyone involved in the trial and did not pull its punches:

1 Molly Davidson in full splendour for her 1910 presentation as a 'Matron' at the Court of St James

2 Harold and Molly Davidson on their wedding day

LEFT 3 The young Harold Davidson at Windsor RIGHT 4 A photo booth image
of Davidson with Barbara Harris, c. 1931. Note the diamond tiepin.

The PERFECT NIPPY

Cap correctly worn,
monogram in centre.

Teeth well cared for.

Clean and well laundered collar
correctly sewn in.

Dress clean and tidy

All buttons sewn on with
red cotton.

Clean and well laundered cuffs,
correctly sewn in.

Point well pressed.

Clean, well laundered apron,
correctly worn.

Dress correct length.

Well polished plain shoes.
Medium heels for comfort.

Ribbon clean and pressed.

No conspicuous use of make-up.
Hair neat and tidy.

Badge clean and securely sewn.

Fastening to have Hooks,
Eyes and Press Studs,
which should be securely
sewn on and fastened.

Clean hands.
Nails well manicured.

Plain Black Stockings.

J. Lyons & Co. Ltd

5 'The Perfect Nippy'. The waitresses at the J. Lyons teahouses were frequent
objects of Davidson's attention.

6 Stiffkey Rectory

7 Major Philip Hamond, c. 1939

8 Rose Ellis

9 Barbara Harris arriving at court

o The trial in the Great Hall of Church House, Westminster. Davidson is on the extreme right with his hand cupped to his ear. The waitress Violet Lowe is giving evidence to Chancellor North's left.

11 Harold Davidson in the pulpit of Stiffkey church, Easter 1932

LEFT 12 Davidson and Betty Beach RIGHT 13 Memorial to Violet Morgan, 'Sweet Vi'.

14 Davison preaching outside the locked Morston church, 10 July 1932

"Best wishes from

Barbara

I took some things to mrs Walton.

15 Last part of a letter from Barbara Harris to Harold Davidson, 20 October 1931

Enquiries can I be made at Wells Station, (about us waiting for two days) for Davidson. Also enquiries can be made from the Garage at (I think) Fackenham or some name like that.

I think my word can be believed.

All this is in Sincerity.

Barbara Harris.

I know. He has the keys of a lot of girls flats, and front Doors.

16 Last part of a letter from Barbara Harris to the Bishop of Norwich, 9 February 1932

It is not to be denied that the long, protracted proceedings of the Stiffkey case, exploited to the nth degree by the popular Press, have been a deplorable incident in recent Church history, and have seriously affected the Church's prestige. We have no hesitation in saying that the conduct of the case by the Bishop's legal advisers was tragically ill-advised. No experienced criminal solicitor could conceivably have blundered so badly and so consistently...[1]

The main tenor of the article was that, under the Clergy Discipline Act of 1892, it was only necessary to prove a single count of immorality against an errant cleric. The prosecution could have accomplished this by calling a few, select witnesses instead of deciding 'to bring forward numerous witnesses of doubtful character and to heap up a number of charges'. Chancellor North, 'who hardly showed himself to be a strong judge', is criticised for agreeing that the trial be held in London instead of Norwich, a decision that 'vastly increased its Press publicity and magnified the scandal'. North is also censured for his lack of compassion towards Davidson: 'A word of real sympathy by the Judge for the ideal which, at least in the beginning of his career, Mr Davidson had set before himself would have raised the Church in the opinion of the masses.'

The publication reserved its most damning criticism for the prosecution and the Bishop of Norwich's inquiry agents. Davidson, it said, was 'throughout foolish and eccentric' but 'is still regarded by many as a champion of the outcast and the wretched'. The bishop's men, by contrast, behaved in a manner that was unchristian:

A Consistory Court is still, in the eyes of the law, a Court Christian. We might at least have expected in it a higher tone than we get in the secular Courts. We did not find it... However necessary the proceedings may have been, the spirit in which they were conducted has shocked the public conscience. The secret enquiry agents, the characters of some of the unnecessary witnesses, above all the photograph, made the trial both undignified and unchristian.[2]

Three days later, on 18 July, Davidson made a triumphant appearance

1 *Church Times* of Friday 15 July 1932.
2 *ibid.*

at the Prince's Cinema in Wimbledon. He was mobbed by a crowd of a thousand people and, before mounting the stage, declared that his desperate financial state had forced him to take up, once again, a profession that he had abandoned some thirty years before. Between screenings of Lupe Velez in the 1930 movie *The Storm*, Davidson performed three variety acts, revived from his youth: the first was a skit on the Norwegian playwright Henrik Ibsen, the second a burlesque of an old-fashioned melodrama and the third an impression of an amateur performance at a school prize day. He went down a storm, taking five or six curtain calls and giving an encore, but within a month the bookings had dried up. Davidson's grandson Colin St Johnston says that the Church approached theatre owners and the press, and exerted their influence to dissuade the former from hiring the rector and the latter from writing about him.

On 30 July the Judicial Committee of the Privy Council, with Lord Atkin presiding, refused Davidson leave to appeal his conviction on questions of fact – in other words, to contest Chancellor North's findings. Davidson was not in court but, after the decision was announced, he told a reporter that he would not give up; he would seek leave to appeal on matters of law.

There followed yet another of the comic interludes for which this affair had become renowned. On 9 August, for an unspecified reason, Davidson was expelled from a nudist camp run by the Harrogate Sunbathing Society. He told reporters that he wanted to establish a similar club among his congregation in Stiffkey.

The next day, Wednesday 10 August, the Registrar of the Norwich Consistory Court, C. B. Bolingbroke, nailed a fourteen-day notice of inhibition on the doors of both the Stiffkey and Morston churches. Dated the previous day, the notice was signed by the Bishop of Norwich and stated that, even though Davidson's application for leave to appeal on matters of law was still pending, he was unfit to minister to his parish:

WHEREAS from the nature of the offences charged against you…it appears to us that great scandal is likely to arise from your continuing to perform the services of the Church while such charges…are under investigation and that your ministration will be useless while such charges…are pending. Now in exercise of the power in this behalf vested in us [by the Clergy Discipline Act of 1892], we do hereby inhibit you the said Harold Francis David-son from performing any services of the Church within our said Diocese of Norwich from and after the expiration of fourteen days from the service of this Notice...

Copies of the inhibition notice were sent to the churchwardens of Morston and Stiffkey and to the rector, still in Harrogate despite his run-in with the grandees of the town's naturist society. He was still in the North on 20 August, performing his music hall act around the provincial theatres. The next day would be his final opportunity, before the notice of inhibition came into force, to take services at Morston and Stiffkey. The *Eastern Daily Press* was there to witness the event – it reported that Davidson travelled all night from Nelson in Lancashire to reach Stiffkey in time to take the morning service. He journeyed in the sidecar of a motorcycle driven by a fellow music-hall artist called Ted Cowin. It poured with rain all night and Davidson was soaked through but there was no time for him to change; he simply donned his robes and entered the church where a congregation of about seventy sat waiting for him.

There were more people standing in the porch and churchyard and women were seen raising handkerchiefs to their eyes as he gave the sermon. There were a thousand people waiting in the road outside the church, according to the paper's reporter, and they thronged about the rector to shake his hand. He told one of the journalists present, 'The loyalty of my parishioners at both Stiffkey and Morston is most wonderful... I shall certainly be at Stiffkey next Sunday.' He was right about Stiffkey but was disastrously wrong about at least one member of his Morston flock.

MAJOR HAMOND'S KICK

The afternoon of 21 August began innocuously enough. Davidson took an afternoon service at Morston church and then decided to drive to Scaldbeck, Philip Hamond's house in Morston, to discuss the arrange-ments for the following Sunday's services. Hamond was now acting churchwarden. Unfortunately, not only had Davidson been barred by the Bishop of Norwich from taking services after the 24th, his old adversary was set on ensuring that the notice of inhibition was enforced. Davidson arrived at Scaldbeck at about 4.30 pm with three friends: his former London landlady Mrs Jessie Walton, a Scotsman called Joseph Henderson and Clinton Gray-Fisk, a church organist and music historian. (According to press reports of the incident, Gray-Fisk was actually in Stiffkey to write an article about Harold Davidson.)

When Davidson rang the bell at Scaldbeck the maid went to fetch the major who emerged shouting 'Get out, you disciple of the Devil!' Davidson tried to calm matters by introducing Gray-Fisk but Hamond told him, 'I don't want to see you or any of your damned pimps!' Davidson then demanded the key to Morston church, to which the major's response was to spin the rector around and push him off the front step with a smart kick to the backside. Gray-Fisk rushed forward to help, shouting to Hamond, 'You damned scoundrel, kicking a gentleman like that with no provocation.' Hamond then turned on Gray-Fisk and gave him the same treatment.

The reasons for Major Hamond's hatred of the rector have been dealt with earlier in this book but there was more to this incident than was reported in the press. According to Hamond's son Richard, who still lives at Scaldbeck, his father later said that what had really enraged him was that the maid had been waving and calling out of the window to Davidson when he pulled up in the car and that the rector had called back to her, as if they were flirting with each other. It was Hamond's misfortune that Davidson and Gray-Fisk decided to press charges of assault; a situation made worse by the fact that the major was a magistrate on the Holt bench.

Major Hamond appeared before the Holt police court on 14 October 1932, charged with two counts of assault. It would have been absurd for Hamond's fellow magistrates to try him and Lord Sandhurst, a magistrate from Cromer, was therefore called in to hear the case. The full extent of the enmity that existed between Davidson and Hamond was laid bare but, in the event, the major proved to be a truthful witness and more or less convicted himself. He admitted applying the toe of his boot to both men and, in the rector's case, described his act as 'a kick of finality and contempt'. He was fined £1 on each count and ordered to pay £6.1s.6d. costs – not a negligible sum for the time. There was no diminution in the level of media interest in Harold Davidson – the national papers were filled with the story, as was the international press. The headline in the *Chicago Tribune*, 'Stiffkey Rector Calls on Major and Gets New Kick', more or less sets the tone for much of the coverage.

What is evident from the public response to Hamond's conviction was that Davidson had become a hate figure in the eyes of many people. The atmosphere of levity that had existed throughout much of his trial had largely evaporated. Many of his parishioners and a section of the public still believed that he had been hard done by, but there were many who considered that he had betrayed the ideals of the Church. After his conviction for assault Major Hamond received an avalanche of letters from wellwishers, many enclosing money towards his fine and others nails to attach to his boots. Richard Hamond told the author that his father received so many cheques and postal orders to help pay his fine that he ended up putting a notice in *The Times*, promising to use the funds to carry out restoration work at Morston church. The letters came from members of the public, from clergymen and churchwardens, from fellow magistrates and from men who had served with the major in the Army. A sampling of their contents reveals the depth of vitriol now being directed at the disgraced rector:

To Major Philip Hamond

Dear Sir,

May we say a word of commendation in reference to enclosed clipping. Your treatment rightly applied, ought to quiet the Rector. He is a disgrace to the church he represents…

Sincerely,
MR AND MRS ALAN HAMMOND
Jersey City
New Jersey
U.S.A.

Dear Sir,

As two direct actionists, we wish to congratulate you most sincerely on your attitude towards the 'Stiffkey Swine'…

To help on the good work we enclose a few nails; these, we suggest should be knocked in the extreme toes of your boots, in clusters of fives: on the off chance of a return visit…

Yours etc…

Dear Sir,

May an Oxfordshire Vicar send you his hearty congratulations for that 'kick of finality and contempt'... It is the one bright spot in a very low down and dirty business.

I hope now that Stiffkey will settle down and forget this most regrettable affair and that Mr D. will join a travelling circus as quickly as possible.

Yours etc...

And this (see illustration 20) from Gerard Gosselin, a fellow parishioner and squire at Hindringham Hall:

Dear Major Hamond,

Allow me to congratulate you... May I suggest that the boot, which did such excellent service to our Church, ought to be presented to the Church and placed in some niche.

Yours etc...

GERARD GOSSELIN

My dear Sir,

Will you please accept my most heartfelt thanks for kicking that insufferable beast Davidson. I am sorry that it cost you £2, but I trust your boots were hard and hefty enough to cause the loathsome creature considerable inconvenience for at least some days...

Yours etc...

Dear Hamond,

Heartfelt congratulations from my wife and myself... My only regret is that I was not there to catch the swine on the rebound...

Yours etc...

CHARLES STOREY
Pensions officer, Church of England
Pensions Board

REMOVED, DEPOSED AND DEGRADED

Harold Davidson's victory at the Holt police court on 14 October was a pyrrhic one. On the previous day the Judicial Committee of the Privy Council had not only dismissed his application for leave to appeal on matters of law, it had awarded costs against him. Davidson wore his dog-collar and represented himself but made no impression at all on Lords Atkin, Tomlin and Wright; they retired for only five minutes before arriving at their judgment. Two memorable details from the hearing were Davidson's declaration that he had originally planned to call 418 witnesses at his trial and, secondly, his utterance of the following statement which seems to go to the root of his difficulties in life: 'The trouble was that I carry into my clerical life the unconventional attitudes of the stage.'

The events of Friday 21 October, an inevitable consequence of the failure of his final appeal, are referred to in the *Eastern Daily Press* as 'The last act in the long drawn out proceedings'. This was the day fixed by the Bishop of Norwich for a sitting of the Consistory Court at Norwich Cathedral, with the purpose of pronouncing sentence on Davidson. The court would sit at 11.45 am and the press were out in force to record each agonising detail of the day's proceedings.

Shortly after 10 am the main body of the cathedral was sealed off, and plain wooden chairs were arranged around a red-baize-covered table in the little Bauchon Chapel, the customary meeting place of the Consistory Court. Numbered among the members of the court were the Bishop of Norwich, Chancellor Keppel North, the Registrar (C. B. Bolingbroke), the Dean (Dr Cranage), Canon A. R. Grant, and the Archdeacons of Norfolk, Norwich and Lynn. Two of the Bishop of Norwich's legal advisors, Walter Monckton and Henry Dashwood, were also present.

The public had also been admitted, although numbers had been limited to the first twelve people in the queue. When 11.45 arrived and proceedings were ready to begin, there was still no sign of the rector; he had managed to be late, even for the dénouement of the case. As the minutes passed there were mutterings among both the public and the assembled worthies until Registrar Bolingbroke stepped forward to announce that a telegram, handed in at Newmarket at 10.22, had just been received by the Bishop of Norwich. It was a classic piece of Davidson theatricality: 'Have motored through night to be present cathedral today eleven forty-five. Have been slightly delayed. If late please allow few minutes' grace. Hope see you and Archdeacon about business matters afterwards. – HAROLD DAVIDSON, rector of Stiffkey.'

Bolingbroke indicated that the proceedings would be delayed until noon to allow Davidson time to arrive and the entire assembly left the chapel, just as what the *Times* correspondent described as a 'small, weather-stained motor-car' pulled up outside. The rector emerged, wearing full clerical garb and a silk top hat and carrying an attaché case. Flanked by his sister Mrs Muriel Cox and a male companion, Davidson raised his hat to a crowd of cheering onlookers and galloped into the Bauchon Chapel to take his seat at the table facing the bishop's throne. There was a brief lull before the Bishop of Norwich and his entourage filed back into the chapel carrying their wands of office, a scene captured by the *Times* correspondent:

> Beyond the low screen forming one side of the chapel could be seen the gold and silver of the Bishop's pastoral staff, and then Dr Pollock entered with his staff in his hand and took his seat on the throne. While the Court remained standing the Apparitor called, 'Oyez, Oyez, Oyez, all persons cited and admonished to appear at this Court draw near and answer to your names as you shall be called. God save the King.' Then came the call for the rector, Harold Francis Davidson, repeated three times, to which he replied, 'Here.'[3]

Bishop Pollock then offered a prayer to those assembled that included the line 'Grant to all Thy servants pardon and peace'. He rose, taking back his staff from his chaplain, and began to read out the sentence. Davidson leapt to his feet and asked if might be allowed to speak before sentence was passed. The bishop assented on condition that he was brief and Davidson stood, staring straight at the bishop with his hands grasping the edge of the red-baize table:

> I wish before you pass sentence to say that I am entirely innocent in the sight of God of any of the graver charges that have been made against me. I have always felt throughout this trial, and it is that which has given me strength to go on, that it is the Church authorities which were on trial and not myself, and whatever my sentence may be I shall work the rest of my life, if God gives me strength and health to do so, towards the reform of the procedure under which these Courts are conducted so that no other clergyman shall suffer

3 *The Times*, Saturday 22 October 1932.

who has striven to do the work which, in my opinion, every clergyman in the Church ought to do, going into the lower depths of
society, leaving the ninety and nine just persons, and going for the
one who is lost. I shall devote myself to that work as I have done
since I was eighteen years of age. There is not one single deed I have
done which I shall not do again with the help of God, if perhaps a
little more discreetly than I have done before. I hope that every clergyman in the Church of England will support me in the campaign
I intend to lead.

Davidson sat down and, without missing a beat, the Bishop of
Norwich stood and began to read out the verdict:

> In the name of God, Amen. Whereas the Judge and Chancellor of
> our Consistory Court has notified to us that the Rev. Harold Fran-
> cis Davidson, M.A., Clerk in Holy Orders, Rector of the parish
> churches of Stiffkey and Morston in our diocese, has been found
> guilty...of certain immoral conduct, immoral acts, and immoral
> habits...and whereas our Chancellor has notified us that the
> sentence of deprivation should be passed...[4] Now we, Bertram, by
> Divine permission Bishop of Norwich...pronounce, decree and
> declare that the Rev. Harold Francis Davidson ought by law to be
> deprived of all his ecclesiastical promotions in the Diocese of
> Norwich, and especially of the Rectory of the parish churches of
> Stiffkey and Morston, of all profits and benefits pertaining to the
> said Rectory, and of any other ecclesiastical promotions in the
> Diocese of Norwich and of the glebe, fruits, tithes, rents, salaries,
> and all other ecclesiastical dues and rights and emoluments...

Pollock then sat down and signed the document he had just read out
before rising again to announce, 'I will now move to the High Altar.'
When he uttered these words Davidson knew at once that he was not
merely to be deprived, he was to be deposed as well. As the bishop
turned to go he leaped up once again, saying 'May I give notice before
the Court that if there is any mode of appeal which the law allows
against this sentence I shall make inquiries and prosecute it.' As the
court rose to make its way to the High Altar, Davidson led the way and

---

4 For the distinctions between deprivation and deposition see page 33.

took a seat in one of the front pews. The bishop's cortège filed solemnly past the rector with Chancellor North wearing what *The Times* rather elegantly described as 'a full-bottomed wig'. The bishop knelt briefly at the High Altar and led prayers, with Davidson and the various dignitaries joining in. He then produced a lengthy document and began to intone its contents in a low voice:

> ...whereas it appears that the said Reverend Harold Francis Davidson has caused grave scandal to the Church and to his Holy Orders, and ought also to be deposed from Holy Orders. Now therefore we, Bertram, by Divine Permission Bishop of Norwich...do thereby pronounce decree and declare that the said Reverend Harold Francis Davidson...ought to be entirely removed, deposed and degraded from the said offices of priest and deacon...

Pollock recited several more prayers, including one that began 'Let Thy continued pity cleanse and defend thy Church', raised his right hand in benediction and then knelt quietly for a moment at the High Altar. As the procession filed past Davidson and moved along the central aisle towards the vestry, he sprang to his feet once again and began to shout in a high-pitched voice. Pollock pointedly ignored him and as he and the other dignitaries progressed along the aisle, the ex-rector of Stiffkey could be heard shrieking:

> I am very glad that the deposition service has been added because I have the right under the Clergy Discipline Act of addressing an appeal to the Archbishop of Canterbury within one month, and with the evidence that has lately come into my possession and for which I asked for ten days' delay to investigate before you sentenced me, I feel confident that the truth will now be divulged and the whole case removed from the atmosphere of misunderstanding and on consideration the sentence reversed.

Regardless of the rights and wrongs of this case there can be few people who have experienced the sort of prolonged, systematic humiliation endured by Harold Davidson throughout much of 1932. He and his family had been lampooned in the popular press, trailed by the bishop's investigators, bankrupted several times over by legal bills, and fêted and reviled by the public in more or less equal measure. To give the Bishop of Norwich his due, there was no air of triumphalism to the proceedings of 21 October. The *Eastern Daily Press* reporter wrote that 'Most who saw and heard left the Cathedral with a deep feeling of sadness' but this did not soften the blows. Davidson had been a minister for twenty-six years but in the space of a few months had lost his name, his livelihood, his pension and his home. At fifty-seven years old he was broken and aged and was about to embark on the final phase of his life as a wandering zealot, on a ceaseless quest to clear his name. There was no hint of this, however, in the interview he gave to a reporter as he left the deposition proceedings. His daughter Paddy had referred to him during her own interview with the *Sunday Dispatch* as an 'India-rubber ball' and there he was, proud and defiant, claiming kinship with the French army officer Alfred Dreyfus:[5]

> I feel intensely that the Church of England, which I have loved and served, and which about twenty-seven of my relatives within the last hundred years also have served as priest, some with distinction, should have been dragged through the mire by this trial. My future plan is to make sufficient money in any way I can to provide funds and take civil action until the whole truth can be revealed. I want to turn the blazing light of truth on the darkest recesses of this case.[6]

The same afternoon Davidson, his sister, a group of supporters and a posse of journalists all headed to Stiffkey so that he could bid farewell to his parishioners. As he toured the village knocking on cottage doors he was upbeat and positive, telling his supporters that he was 'not done yet' and was still hopeful of a successful appeal to the Archbishop of Canterbury. By 11 pm, his dog collar now replaced by a neat butterfly number, Davidson was ready for an overnight drive to Blackpool. He promised to be back to 'carry on his ministerial duties' and his business manager Mr G. Clarke told a reporter that they would be sailing within a few weeks for a lecture tour of America. While they were there, he

5 Captain Alfred Dreyfus (1859 –1935) was wrongly convicted of treason in 1894, largely because of anti-Semitism in the French Army. He was finally exonerated in 1906, only after a vigorous campaign on his behalf by the author Emile Zola and others. In his 1936 pamphlet *I Accuse* Davidson clearly identifies with the open letter *J'Accuse,* written by Zola to the President of France in defence of Dreyfus.
6 Harold Davidson, quoted in the *Eastern Daily Press* of 22 October 1932.

said, Davidson would be making talking pictures. They had also been inundated with offers, he added, to appear in various parts of the UK and in Europe. Much of this, of course, was pie in the sky. Harold Davidson was destined to spend most of his remaining years as a sideshow freak on the Blackpool Promenade.

8

Cleric in a Cask

Even before the Bishop of Norwich pronounced his verdict on 21 October, Harold Davidson had already made his début on Blackpool's Golden Mile. He first appeared at the beginning of September, booked by a local impresario called Luke Gannon. He offered Davidson £500 to fast, Diogenes-like, in a barrel for fourteen days.[1] The barrel was custom-built with a padded seat, a window at the side for addressing his audience and a chimney for the rector's cigar smoke.

Luke Gannon, known as the 'Blackpool Barnum', was one of the Golden Mile's most successful and controversial showmen. He came to Blackpool from Burnley in 1924 after a spell as a weaver and quickly made his name as a promoter of sideshows of somewhat questionable taste. One of his early successes was Daisy Winterbottom, billed as 'the Ugliest Woman in the World', who slept in a pit of monkeys and snakes. Gannon offered £1,000 to anyone who would marry her but there were no takers. Another of his stunts was to fool a local primary school into enrolling a twenty-year-old woman in a class of ten-year-olds, but his speciality, 'The Starving Brides and Bridegrooms', made him the largest amount of money for the longest period. According to local historian Cyril Critchlow in his book *Blackpool's Golden Mile*, even Gannon's funeral was a piece of theatre when he died in October 1939. He had given instructions that no clergyman be permitted to speak and the mourners sat in silence until, at last, his coffin rolled out through the curtains of the crematorium to the strains of Chopin's Funeral March.

Davidson's act created a sensation: on the first day a crowd of somewhere between 2,000 and 10,000 people (depending on which report

---

1 Diogenes of Sinope (born c. 400 BC) was a member of the Cynics, a Greek philosophical sect that eschewed luxury and placed great emphasis on self-sufficiency. His disdain for life's comforts led him, at one stage, to take up residence in a tub. In one – probably apocryphal – account Alexander the Great is said to have sought out Diogenes and asked him what service he might offer him. Diogenes replied 'Get out of my light.'

one reads) paid twopence a head to file past the barrel, blocking the traffic on the promenade. Davidson could be seen working on papers for his next appeal, writing letters or giving speeches to the crowd. He wasn't the only freak-show at Blackpool, nor was he the only person fasting in a barrel. The *Blackpool Gazette and Herald* of 17 September 1932 describes a fasting contest between the occupants of two other barrels – a young woman and a youth who, it was claimed, had gone without solid food for a year.

Davidson also shared the billing, the paper reported, with Mariana 'the gorilla girl', Susi 'the girl with the elephant skin', at least one mermaid and, as a counterpoint to all the fasting, there was Dick Harrow 'the world's fattest man'. Madame Polanowski 'the bearded lady of Russia', Jo-Jo 'the dog-faced man', Frisco 'the three-legged boy of Italy' and Yanika 'the bird-faced man' were also appearing that week. The ignominy of it all was not lost on Davidson. The remarks he made to a reporter from the *Blackpool Gazette* also contain the gist of what he told the gawpers who paid to file past his barrel: 'Every fibre of my being revolts against the indignity of this procedure but desperate ills require desperate remedies and I am prepared to go on with it. My bishop has pilloried me before the world as a most objectionable character and a menace to decent living people. I would rather be charged with murder. I have lived a clean life and upheld high ideals.'

Les Prager, interviewed for BBC radio programme *A Proper Little Gent*, saw Davidson's barrel performance during the summer of 1933 and thought it utterly sordid and undignified:

> He was very tatty and the place stank... You could peep in at this poor devil in his clerical grey lying on a camp-bed...every so often he'd look up, nod to the people and smile, and close his eyes in resignation. Every half hour he would climb out from his barrel, straighten his jacket, light a cigarette and hand out pamphlets, and say 'Good evening, good evening. Would you care to read my life story? Not everything you read about me is true.' He spoke in a terrible far-back monotone.

The Blackpool Corporation thought it undignified too; within days of his appearance (and before his deposition in Norwich Cathedral) they prosecuted both Davidson and Gannon for obstruction. They appeared before Blackpool magistrates on 10 September and were discharged on condition that they discontinued the barrel stunt. Any notion on the part of the authorities that this would curtail the publicity-seeking antics of either man was naïve, to say the least.

On the eve of their court appearance the *Blackpool Gazette and Herald* interviewed them both, the article appearing on the 10th. Davidson told the reporter that he would fight his case and added, apparently without irony, that he was attracting so many extra visitors to the town that he was thinking of asking the railway company for a concession. He had shaken hands with no fewer than 3,200 people that day and 750 of them said that they had come to town especially to see him. He and Gannon had been served their summonses at the studios of the Northern Regional Film Corporation in the Blackpool suburb of Bispham, where they were busy making a film about the rector's barrel exploits. The rector, in flannel suit, trilby and button boots, twirled a cane before lighting a cigar and launching into a monologue entitled 'What is Life?' As the camera rolled he spoke about what the *Gazette* refers to as 'the philosophy of the birds and flowers'. The film does not appear to have survived.

Contrition was not to be the strong point of either man. They were both determined to wring all they could from Davidson's notoriety – literally indeed to milk it. Luke Gannon's only regret, he told the *Gazette*, was that the Blackpool court proceedings had interrupted his plan to have the rector fast in his barrel for three days and nights, with nothing to sustain him but a famous brand of milk that they had presumably been paid to endorse.

Davidson meanwhile, at this point still to be defrocked, was strolling around Blackpool with large crowds in tow; buying cigars, signing autographs and firing off telegrams to Stiffkey. At this stage, it should be remembered, he was no longer permitted to preach but was still returning each Sunday to address those parishioners who remained loyal in the grounds of the Stiffkey rectory. After 21 October he was finished as a priest and became a permanent fixture on the Golden Mile. Despite his assurances to the Blackpool court the barrel act quickly resumed and was to sustain him until 1936.

A great favourite with Davidson's audience were the large numbers of postcards that he had had printed in support of his cause. With titles like 'STRANGE BUT TRUE!' and 'FACTS FOR INTELLIGENT-MINDED RE: THE GREAT STIFFKEY RECTOR SCANDAL', they were distributed in large numbers and contained the basic facts of the case. The allegations were the same as those that were made at the trial: that the case was a colossal waste of public money, that Barbara was bribed and that Rose was plied with drink. A pliant Barbara, one of the cards claimed, had been so utterly corrupted by a 'couple of scallywag divorce detectives' that she 'was almost prepared to extend her jaws to breaking point'. He claimed to have unearthed 'entirely new evidence' which would constitute a 'bombshell… blowing up the wall of lies built up by the prosecution'.

Davidson did not merely confine himself to barrels. In one variant he was locked in a refrigerated chamber, vowing that he would freeze himself to death to shame the dark forces that had brought him to his current state. In another stunt he appeared to be roasting in an enclosed pit while a mechanical imp prodded his buttocks with a gilded pitchfork. The placard for this particular routine has survived in photographs and reads:

> WELL I'LL GO TO — — [Cartoon drawing of hell]!
> STARVING FREEZING NOW ROASTING
> Ex Stiffkey Rector is Here in Person
> 2d. Admission

On another placard to accompany the same act he compared himself to Joan of Arc: condemned to burn by a cruel, inhuman Church. The fact that he was to be seen most evenings enjoying a cigar and strolling along the Blackpool Promenade does not appear to have dented his credibility very much. He sent a telegram to Mahatma Gandhi at one point, inviting him to come to Blackpool to sit in his barrel. Davidson's rather melodramatic view of his predicament was apparent from the sign at the entrance to the exhibit:

THE FORMER RECTOR OF STIFFKEY HAS BEEN PLACED IN HIS PRESENT POSITION BY THE AUTHORITIES OF THE CHURCH OF ENGLAND WHO FAILED IN THEIR CHRISTIAN DUTY TOWARDS HIM AT THE VERY MOMENT WHEN, GUILTY OR INNOCENT, THEIR RESPONSIBILITY TO HIM BECAME GREATEST. THE LOWER HE SINKS, THE GREATER THEIR CRIME.[2]

2 Recounted by Davidson in his 1936 pamphlet, *I Accuse.*

It may have been degrading, but it was lucrative too. In *I Accuse* Davidson states that even during the summer season of 1936, when interest in his antics was waning, no fewer than 174,345 people paid to see him perform in his barrel. At twopence a head this would have netted Davidson and Luke Gannon £1,452 between them, a considerable sum for the time. Not very much of it seems to have stuck to the rector's hands, however; Gannon seems to have been the principal beneficiary of his stunts.

The *West Lancashire Evening Gazette* interviewed Luke Gannon's cashier, a Mrs Lily Pilkington, in 1982. Lily was the sister of one of Gannon's most successful acts, a beautiful mind-reader with the stage name of 'Madam Kusharny'. People did not forget Harold Davidson easily and Lily Pilkington was no exception; despite the passage of fifty years her recollections were still vivid. She told one story about his false teeth: apparently he left them on his plate while eating in a café and they were thrown out with the leftovers. She also described a rather cruel trick played on the rector involving a Bob Martin's Dog Powder. He had complained of fatigue one day, in the same café, and was fed one of the tonics as a joke. Within half an hour he was rushing for the bathroom and that evening's performance had to be cancelled. Davidson was also the subject of quite a few drinking songs in and around Blackpool and Lily had written down the words of one of them:

> Oh Mr Stiffkey, what will we do with you?
> You've upset all the place, you know, and made a right to-do.
> Will you get out of Blackpool, as fast as ever you can?
> Oh Mr Stiffkey, sir, you are a naughty man.
> The Old Hens' Association held a meeting on the sands
> And passed a note of censure by holding up their hands.
> They marched off to the barrel – it was 12 o'clock at night,
> Their tonsils were quite out of tune
> But they yelled with all their might:
> Oh Mr Stiffkey...[3]

3 Quoted by Mrs Lily Pilkington in the *West Lancashire Evening Gazette* of 24 September 1982. It was probably inevitable that Davidson would become known as 'Mr Stiffkey'. One could argue that a major reason why the scandal is so well remembered is because of the faintly salacious sound of the village name. Tom Cullen refers to it as 'priapic' and perhaps it is just as well that Davidson was not also rector of the adjacent village, Cockthorpe.

There were signs that, in some quarters at least, public sympathy was turning against him. He was pilloried in an editorial in the *Sunday Express*: in an article entitled 'Stupidity That Only Advertises Him', the opinion was expressed that 'the rector of Stiffkey would soon be forgotten if the police and bishops could be persuaded to abandon their booming of his absurdities'. Davidson's harebrained activities in Blackpool at least meant that he could keep body and soul together but the forces of law and order were not far behind him.

In June 1933 his former landlady, the formidable Mrs Flora Osborne who had given evidence at his trial, successfully sued him for £43 in unpaid rent. Bailiffs arrived at his sideshow to deliver the court's judgment order and were treated to a virtuoso performance from the old thespian. He asked if he could have a moment to shake hands with some of his supporters and then sped off on foot along the Golden Mile towards his rooms. According to one of the bailiffs, a man called J. P. Oldroyd, as they banged on the front door of his lodgings Davidson climbed down a drainpipe at the rear and escaped. He gave himself up later in the day and was sentenced to nine days in prison in Liverpool. On his release, Oldroyd recalls, the rector returned to Blackpool in an open carriage accompanied by two African women who threw flowers to the crowd. When he arrived back in the town he was welcomed by a bassoon band.

Joan Sternberg, one of his former parishioners who died in 1994, remembered Davidson's trial and subsequent downfall with great clarity. In her account of a childhood spent in Stiffkey village[4] she alludes to a trial by media that left Davidson a laughing stock throughout Britain:

> I shall not forget, nor forgive, that picture, the ignominy of it all. The Church (I thought, as a teenager) was behaving in a most unseemly and unchristian way. Where was the forgiveness, the mercy, the help the Rector certainly needed just then? Instead, the treatment meted out to him by the Church and the public (for we were also to blame) simply drove the poor man to new excesses.

There was a further erosion of public sympathy in October 1933. In an article in the *Blackpool Gazette and Herald* headlined 'Blackpool's

---

4 Joan Sternberg, *Don't Tread on the Butterflies: Memoirs of a Childhood in Heacham and Stiffkey, 1912–1932*, Dereham: Norfolk, Larks Press, 2000.

Biggest Blot', the sideshows of the town's Central Beach attract serious criticism. The paper's reporter tours them and is shocked by what he sees. These were the David Blaines of the day – their antics a bizarre mix of the erotic and the grotesque:

Fantastic freak-shows of all kinds pander to the most morbid streak in holiday-makers, and it cannot be said that Central Beach in its present form is a credit to Blackpool... There is a man crucified on a cross. There are girls fasting in barrels. He who was the Rector of Stiffkey is there, and there, too, are models in wax of creatures out of Grand Guignol... Beyond the cash desk is a case of wood with a glass roof. Inside, at the foot of the long, low bed is a litter of crumpled magazines, empty siphons, discarded cigarette packets. On the bed is a girl. She is pretty, not embarrassed by the gaping curiosity of the people who walk in procession past her hour after hour...

'Five days are gone; another twenty-seven.' Her voice through the glass roof of her chosen penitentiary is faint and a little hoarse... She has been in the case for five days. If she remains in it she will be paid £300. So the showman announces. He announces, too, that when the case was sealed there was left in it six siphons of soda water, six siphons of lemonade, 250 cigarettes...

The showman advances to the front of the tiny shallow stage... 'Mavourneen!' he announces, sweeps back the curtain, reveals a mountain of a woman in a shapeless blue print dress who, when she smiles, discloses a row of jagged teeth, who, when she stands, bulges and trembles with fat. She is 33, born in Ireland, 33 stone in weight, and...cannot sit on one chair, and so squats as an alternative on a cushioned plank between two chairs...

The curtain is drawn again. They forget Mavourneen. For here is La Belle Eve, posing in a dress not a little abbreviated. Not that La Belle Eve is inclined to be apologetic about that, for, as she explains in a strange, Anglo-French patois, 'It is in Paris so different – for *zere* –.' La Belle Eve indicates that there the authorities do not require the dress, however abbreviated, at all.

And all that costs 2d.

There is a merry little man in a nearby show. They call him Tiny Tim. He was 46 the other day... Tiny Tim struts inside an enclosure, a doll's house without a roof, day after day. People tower over him, leaning on the enclosure's walls… Outside the profession he is Alf Pyott. He weighs 24lb. He is an inch short of two feet in height…

But folks, you ain't seen nothing yet… Here is a man crucified. He is hanging limp on a cross. Silver spikes pierce his flesh to the wood. He was there twelve hours the other day and 8,700 people passed the cash desk to see him. The strange story he tells is that a savage tribe took him prisoner as he was preaching the Gospel in the South Seas, that they nailed him to a tree, that another tribe, delivering him from death, anointed the wounds with an ointment unknown to medical science.

It is through the old wounds, impervious to pain under the magic ointment's ministrations, that the silver spikes nail him to his cross on the Blackpool Promenade. 'A religious man he is, too,' protests the showman who exhibits him. 'He's earning this money only so that he can go back to the South Seas and be a missionary again.'

Twelve hours they think is a little too long for him to endure. They have reduced it to six lately, although Mr Harold Davidson has been on view in the same show right around the clock…

On the second floor of an arcade is a man in 'The Tomb of Death'. Raymond Tac, immaculately undisturbed, lies in a coffin inside another glass case, a coffin of which the sides are draped with white embroidered lace.

Unemotional, utterly self-assured is Raymond Tac in his coffin, gazing up through eyes shielded by big horn-rimmed glasses, his face lean and intelligent.

'How long have you been there, Mr Tac?' I asked him.

'Oh, just twelve days,' he said…

The crowd passes, gazes curiously, pays its twopence and takes its choice – the man on the cross, the wife of Goliath, the fasting girls. They're all here.

Beat that drum! Roll up! Roll up![5]

A year later, in 1934, Davidson was still there, as were the shows

[5] Abridged from the *Blackpool Gazette and Herald* of 21 October 1933.

which, if anything, had become even more tasteless. Davidson's dignity was not spared by a recording made that year by the music hall comedian Charlie Higgins. The song was called 'Charlie Makes Whoopee' and contained the line 'There was an old parson of Stiffkey, whose actions spoke louder than words'. The record was produced by the Crystalate Gramophone Company and distributed by Marks and Spencer. Davidson sued them both for £200 and won. The record was withdrawn from sale.

In October there was another storm – this time precipitated by the visit of Lord Mottistone to Blackpool for a National Savings Conference. It appears that he was outraged by the freak shows along the Golden Mile and demanded that the town council do something about them. What particularly appalled him was Luke Gannon's latest innovation, 'The Starving Brides and Bridegrooms' of Central Beach. The mayor of Blackpool sent in the police on 13 October with instructions to shut Gannon down. Three separate shows of starving brides and grooms, one operated by Gannon, were ordered to close. The occupants of the three sets of coffins were woken up, examined by a doctor and prescribed a diet of brandy, milk and eggs.

Gannon was incandescent; he would fight any attempt to prosecute him and demanded that Lord Mottistone come and pay the £250 he had pledged to each couple that completed a thirty-day fast. Without a trace of irony, Gannon exclaimed that not only had he paid £250 to the previous couple that had fasted in the cabinet but paid the 'convalescence fees' as well. Within days two of the three shows, including Gannon's couple who had refused to break their fast, were back in business.

Harold Davidson was nowhere to be seen during all of this although he did put in an appearance the following week to voice his support for Gannon in his battle with the town council. Despite the mayor's attempts to close the shows, and despite vigorous protests by the local church, all that was actually accomplished was a lot of press attention that attracted even more people to the Golden Mile. The shows were closed voluntarily at the end of the month when the season ended but Gannon and his fellow showmen vowed to be back the following year.

Before the 1935 season began the Blackpool town council drafted an 'Improvement Act' that would empower them to deal with 'offensive and objectionable side shows and exhibitions'. Madame Tussaud's secured an exclusion from the new act for waxwork dummies. The law did not receive Royal Assent until 2 August and, as a result, the summer season began as outrageously as before. Davidson was there once again at Gannon's invitation – this time disporting himself in a glass coffin with a placard that read: 'The ex-Rector of Stiffkey claims that he will make it his Life's End and will Fast unto Death if his appeal is unheeded.'

For the 1935 season Davidson had agreed to fast for ten days and then spend twenty-four hours encased in ice. He had also arranged with Gannon to perform in Blackpool and Newcastle with a somewhat unusual prop. With the rector presumably taking the role of Jonah, he was to be accompanied by a stuffed whale. (The performance with the stuffed, or as Davidson called it the 'mummified', whale went ahead in both cities as planned. Davidson refers to it in the statement for counsel that he prepared for his 1935 civil action against the Blackpool Corporation.)

The 'Improvement Act' served only to revive flagging public interest in the rector and on 3 August, just after the law had come into force, he was in the newspapers once again. The police had been dispatched to Luke Gannon's premises, only to encounter waxwork effigies of Jack the Ripper and a Negro minstrel flanking the entrance. As a registered waxworks exhibit, the police were informed, Gannon's show could not be closed. After an all-night meeting at the town hall a new strategy was formulated: it was decided that Davidson would be prosecuted for attempted suicide. He was removed from his glass coffin and escorted to the police station clutching, the press reported, a copy of the Bible and a cigar. There was certainly no hint of contrition in his remarks to reporters: 'I am glad this has happened for I think it will bring the bishop to his senses.' The bishop was unmoved and Davidson was charged with 'unlawfully fasting with intent to feloniously, wilfully and of malice aforethought kill and murder himself'. For once the law was on the rector's side. A doctor gave evidence at the trial to the effect that after ten days in his coffin he had emerged in a better state of health than when he had gone in – 'The rest had done him good.' Davidson was acquitted and later received damages of £382 from the Blackpool Corporation for wrongful imprisonment. His statement to counsel during the civil action against the Blackpool Corporation contains interesting details about his life during these difficult years.

On 20 November he was in the newspapers yet again. He attended a

Church Assembly meeting at Central Hall, Westminster, at which Dr Cosmo Gordon Lang, the Archbishop of Canterbury, was present. He stood up in the public gallery and demanded that he be allowed to state his case. Dr Lang forbade him to address the meeting, at which point he cut the string securing a large bundle of pamphlets and let them shower down onto the delegates below before fleeing the building with stewards in pursuit.

Davidson's pamphlet entitled *I Accuse* has already been touched upon. It contains the rector's declaration of his innocence and sets out his case against those who brought him down. He criticises Pollock, Searle, Dashwood, North and Lang and demands that the 1892 Clergy Discipline Act be repealed, that his case be re-examined and that he be reinstated as rector of Stiffkey. He reserves a special disdain for Christopher Searle, whom he accuses of 'lying, misrepresentation, bribery and corruption of witnesses' and Chancellor Keppel North, whose principal attributes were 'judicial incapacity, physical disability, rank prejudice and occasional somnolence'. On the last page he gives the Church authorities an ultimatum: either they grant him a fresh trial or he will attempt to have the Bishop of Norwich's legal advisors and investigators, as well as Philip Hamond's wife and his former landlady Mrs Alice Lake, put on trial for criminal conspiracy.

There is an increasing air of desperation to the rector's tactics at the end of 1936. He wrote a letter to Keppel North[6] immediately after the Church Assembly incident, enclosing a copy of the *I Accuse* pamphlet. His strategy is laid bare in the letter: if the claims he makes in the pamphlet are true, he declares, then his case should be re-examined by the Church authorities and, if they are false, he should be prosecuted and imprisoned for libel. Either outcome would have to be decided in court and each would provide the rector with a public platform on which to argue his case and present the new evidence that he claimed to possess. He was, he said, 'thoroughly tired of the present position of two-thirds of the world thinking me innocent and one-third thinking me guilty'. A letter to Mrs Lake,[7] his former landlady and a key

6 Letter from Harold Davidson to F. Keppel North, 23 November 1936.
7 Letter from Harold Davidson to Mrs Alice Lake, 23 November 1936. Davidson also wrote on the same day in a similar vein to the Archbishop of Canterbury, the Bishop of Norwich, Mrs Philip Hamond, Henry Dashwood, and Graham Heath, one of the bishop's legal advisors.

prosecution witness, is written on the same day and its message is clear: she and her husband must retract the evidence they gave in the 1932 trial or suffer the consequences. He repeats the claim that he made during the trial, that it was the Lakes who induced Barbara to write her letter to the Bishop of Norwich. He refers to an impending libel action he was taking against *John Bull* magazine for a defamatory article it had written about him. Again, his intention appears to have been to provoke a public trial in which he could present new evidence that might exonerate him.

9
Harold Davidson's Last Adventure

When Harold Davidson gatecrashed the meeting of the Church Assembly in Westminster in November 1936 the incident attracted a few reports in the national newspapers but it was clear that the public was losing interest in his case. Davidson was on his uppers. One of the worst consequences of the trial was that Chancellor North had awarded costs against him. He was living in South Harrow in a small house purchased by his wife with the proceeds of life insurance policies. He existed on handouts from friends (most notably from his solicitor Glynn Barton), by pawning what remained of his possessions and by borrowing £50 from the Ecclesiastical Commissioners.[1] His performances in Blackpool were confined to the summer months and in winter he worked in various odd jobs. In a letter in Colin St John-ston's possession, written by Davidson on 11 March 1937 and addressed to 'My dear Lord Bishop' (presumably the Bishop of Bradford or London), he refers to his various attempts to make ends meet over the previous six months. He had applied unsuccessfully to work for a 'Mr Selfridge' (presumably Selfridge's Department Store) and had that day earned £1 commission selling copies of the *Oxford Dictionary*, *Pictorial Knowledge* and Winston Churchill's latest works. He even worked as a porter at London's St Pancras Station. In her account of her grandfather's life, Karilyn Collier quotes from a notebook kept by Molly in which she describes a pitiful encounter with her husband at St Pancras:

[1] The Ecclesiastical Commissioners were set up by Parliament in 1836 to reorganise dioceses, abolish surplus posts in cathedrals and take over both the responsibility for funding bishops and some cathedral costs, and the assets that had supported those responsibilities. The surplus income was to be used 'for the cure of souls in parishes where such assistance is most required'. They had a major role in financing churches for the new population centres that grew up in the Industrial Revolution and in supporting the stipends of the clergy who worked there. In 1856 they took over the work of the Church Building Commissioners and from 1907 they became involved with clergy pensions. (Abridged from the Church Commissioners for England website.)

I met him one day at St Pancras station, he had got himself a job as a porter. He smiled at me and said 'I've earned 3s. 4d today helping people with their luggage.' He showed me the money he had in his pocket, then he did a funny walk to show me how he grappled with their cases. There was this man who had devoted his whole life to alleviating the world's pain and suffering, cast out...[2]

Davidson did at least seem to be on the brink of more dignified and gainful employment, but there followed, in November 1936, an unfortunate incident at Victoria Station. It was claimed that he had accosted two sixteen-year-old girls, one a kiosk attendant, and offered them £5 each to audition for a part in a forthcoming West End play. The girls reported him to the police and when he returned the next day he was arrested on a charge of 'trespassing on railway property', which was apparently a euphemism for importuning.

Davidson was outraged; he could explain his presence at the station, he said. A young actress had asked him to hear her read a part in a play that she hoped to perform in and he had broken his journey at Victoria to meet her. He had given up his ticket at the barrier and before he had walked more than a few yards the police had arrested him. The arrest had put paid to his attempts to find respectable work. His insistence that there was a perfectly innocent explanation for his behaviour was rejected by the magistrate at the Westminster police court and he was fined a total of £7.8s (including costs). He offered to pay off his fine at the rate of one shilling per week although the court costs would have to wait until he had repaid the money that he had borrowed from his friends. The magistrate was not impressed: he ordered Davidson to repay the full £7.8s. within a month or go to prison for fifteen days.

The rector was driven to new levels of desperation. Although he was fearful of animals – even cows, dogs and mice – in the winter of 1936 he agreed to a series of performances to begin the following summer at a Skegness amusement park. He would be performing in a cage, initially with a single lion, under the supervision of a sixteen-year-old part-Chinese lion tamer called Irene Violet Somner, or 'La Rena' as she was

2 Molly Davidson, quoted in Karilyn Collier, *Harold Francis Davidson, Rector of Stiffkey: A Biography of His Life and Trial*, Zevrika Publications, 2004.

known to her audience. There is a brief article in the *Skegness News* of 9 June 1937, referring to the imminent arrival in the town of 'possibly the most discussed person in the world in recent years'.

The photographs that survive of Davidson's performances in the lions' cage are affectingly poignant. Here is a man completely out of his depth. In one photograph he stands with a whip in one hand and a cigar in the other, and in another is armed only with a walking stick and a copy of the speech that he would be delivering to his audience.

The event was organised by 'Captain' Fred Rye, who invited David-son in the summer of 1937 to stay with him and his family at Poplar Farm in Burgh, Lincolnshire. Rye's daughter Mrs Betty Lucas[3] was a child of eight when Davidson came to stay. The rector was welcomed into the family and was especially fond of young Betty. He even brought his barrel with him from Blackpool, Betty recalls – it remained on the farm for years before it finally disintegrated.

Rye bred a variety of exotic animals at Poplar Farm: Betty grew up with pigs, sheep, ponies, monkeys, a honey bear, a panther, a leopard, snakes, vultures, zebras, various lions and a five-legged cow called Gracie, bought by the captain from a freak-show in Blackpool. A copy of his performing animals licence for October 1936 also reveals that he owned six wolves. He had run away to join a circus as a boy and, after a spell as a coal miner, came to settle in Skegness immediately after the First World War. Rye was asthmatic and the sea air was therapeutic. He set up a carting business in the town and before long had made enough money to purchase Poplar Farm. He had a way with animals and began a lucrative collaboration with Harold Bostock of Bostock and Womb-well's Travelling Menagerie. Bostock provided Rye with exotic animals for breeding stock and Rye would use them to ensure a steady supply for his friend's stage acts around the country and his own show on the Skegness Promenade. He was also a friend of the holiday camp magnate Billy Butlin and provided a sanctuary for the animals from Butlin's zoo during the Second World War. The war brought his animal act to an end, however. There were no performances after 1939 and he gradually sold off his animals as the war progressed, partly because of the difficulties of obtaining food to sustain them and partly because people had lost their appetite for frivolities of this kind. In 1946 he sold

3 Interviews with the author 18 February 2004 and 17 February 2005.

Poplar Farm and moved into Skegness town, remaining there until his death in 1955.

By all accounts Captain Rye was a ladies' man and Betty Lucas recalls that Sunday morning gatherings at Poplar Farm were well attended by the ladies and socially rather select. Rye would give them a private tour of his menagerie and some of the whispering arising from these visits suggests that he and Davidson had similar susceptibilities.

He first met Davidson on the Blackpool Promenade in 1935 or 1936 and seems to have had little trouble in persuading the rector to move to Skegness. It would be wrong to think that Captain Rye exploited Davidson; he was a welcome guest in the Rye household and was clearly excited to be performing in Skegness. In a letter written to Rye in June 1937, it is clear that he considers Skegness to have been a significant step-up on Blackpool:

> Dear Captain Rye,
>
> I felt I must just write a short line to tell you how very happy I am to be working with you during this season in Skegness, and I hope our association may last well beyond that…
>
> I am extremely pleased with the dignified way in which you and Mr Wallace are putting over the show, and I think Skegness itself quite a delightful place to be in, especially after the blatant vulgarity of Blackpool.
>
> When writing to the Bishop of London last night, I said that I had been happier during the last week-end than I had been at any time since the beginning of my Consistory Court Trial.
>
> Yours sincerely,
>
> HAROLD DAVIDSON[4]

Rye actually used four lions – two males and two females – during his performances at Sea View Esplanade, Skegness. His act took place in a large cage, partitioned in two, with a male and female in each section. All, including a male lion called Freddie and a female named Toto, were docile and Betty Lucas remembers going into the cage with her father on many occasions. Davidson performed with a single lion

---

4 Letter from Harold Davidson to Captain Fred Rye, 16 June 1937. Letter in the possession of Rye's daughter Mrs Betty Lucas. The 'Mr Wallace' referred to in the letter is Davidson's manager Norman Wallace.

right through the summer; it was only in July that he began to perform with both Freddie and Toto in the same cage. Initially he was said to have been far from happy with the two-lion arrangement but appears to have quickly settled into a routine – Diogenes had turned into Daniel.

It would be wrong to suppose that Davidson's spirit had been broken by the events of the preceding five years. It was true that his finances were in a desperate state but he remained as determined as ever to clear his name. He gave a brief interview to the *Skegness News*, published on 14 July, in which he declared that he was about to leave for London to consult with his solicitors about another appeal against his 1932 conviction and sentence. The newspaper reported that more people than ever had been to see the rector performing at Rye's pavilion, including a large number of clergymen from all over the country. Many of them had stayed behind after the show to speak to him. 'It shows their sympathy with the attitude I have adopted,' Davidson told the paper.

Until the early 1920s Skegness was a small, unprepossessing coastal town with a couple of churches and an eighteenth-century inn. Apart from a rather tenuous connection to the poet Tennyson (his family occasionally holidayed there), it was hardly a cultural magnet and amenities were meagre. Few visitors came to the town. Things changed in 1922, when the local council purchased the entire seafront area from the Earl of Scarbrough for £15,000. An intense development programme was then undertaken between 1922 and 1937, transforming the town into one of the country's busiest holiday resorts. Esplanades, boating lakes, gardens, ballrooms, restaurants, bathing pools and bowling greens were all laid out, the old Victorian pier was modernised and by the time Harold Davidson arrived in 1937 the town was booming. Rail links to the big industrial towns of the Midlands were excellent, and many factories ceased production for two weeks in the summer while most of their workforce took their families off to Skegness. Billy Butlin opened his first holiday camp there in 1936 and the crowds of holidaymakers along North Parade and Scarborough Esplanade were entertained by the likes of Fred Beck's Modern Follies, the Julie Rodgers Orchestra and Daredevil Leslie the diver, who would leap off the end of the pier. For the bands of roving photographers in their bright orange-striped blazers, business was brisk and there were always trippers with money to spend with showmen like Fred Rye. Beside the lion act and the five-legged cow, Captain Rye's other shows included an attractive blonde who lay on a cot surrounded by animals[5] and Captain ('Was He Man or Woman?') Barker.

Harold Davidson wrote what must have been his last letter on 27 July 1937. The recipient was Mrs Rye, Captain Rye's wife, and the letter contained a small gift for little Betty. In it Davidson retains his customary disdain for convention: he was, he reported, 'only 25 minutes late' for his appearance that day at the Westminster police court in London. He was in court for failing to pay the £7.8s. in fines and costs imposed for the Victoria Station incident the previous November. When he arrived, he wrote, he had been surprised to see Captain Rye sitting at the back of the court. He was hopeful that the Westminster case could be settled amicably; the implication contained in the letter being that Rye and the rector's manager Norman Wallace would settle the fine, presumably with a loan against his future earnings.

Davidson was hounded and humiliated right to the end of his life and this, his last court appearance, was no exception. The events leading up to it were as madcap and as enveloped in publicity as ever. On 21 July two Skegness policemen, Inspector Harvey and Sergeant Withers, had shown up at Captain Rye's pavilion with a warrant to arrest him for non-payment of the Westminster fine. The press had got wind of the latest Davidson 'scoop' and were in attendance to hear the rector tell the two policemen that, if they wanted to arrest him, they would have to come into the lion's cage. A standoff ensued before Davidson emerged and was led off to the police station.

The *Skegness News* of 4 August 1937 reported the Westminster police court proceedings in great detail. Davidson took the stand to describe at length the difficulties he had faced during the past years – it was almost as if he were reciting his own obituary. He was outraged that the warrant had been executed at his place of work; as a result of which he might well lose a job that was the only thing between him and his wife and penury. His financial troubles originated, he claimed, not with his fatuous investments with Arthur Gordon but with his courageous, single-handed but ultimately failed campaign on behalf of the

5 See illustration 24.

whole of the tithe-owning clergy to be spared the local council's rates that were levied on their income. He may have disputed the details but what is undeniable is that in November 1925 Davidson was unable to pay his rates and consequently found himself first threatened with jail, and then declared bankrupt. After losing his livelihood entirely after the trial of 1932 and with debts of several hundred pounds, he said, he had turned to his old profession to eke out a living. After only two weeks of stage work he had been blacklisted, first by the Variety Artists Federation and next by the Cinematograph Union, and wound up as a sideshow exhibit: 'Baulked of every dignified and legitimate way of earning a living, [I] had no alternative but to fall into the hands of showmen, who had exploited [me] very satisfactorily from their own point of view, and by means of which [I] had earned sufficient money, at any rate, to keep [me] going until last October.'[6]

The demands of the Westminster police court on 27 July 1937 may have cost Harold Davidson his life. In his last letter to Mrs Rye, he said that he would be in Skegness by 9.15 am the next morning. He must therefore have left London in the small hours, distracted by both financial and legal worries. He was in the lion enclosure at Rye's Pavilion by 10 am with little or no sleep, which will have done nothing for his already well-documented unease with animals. He then had to carry out a series of performances that required great concentration before a crowd of holidaymakers. What happened next was documented in all its ghastly detail in the newspaper reports of the inquest – particularly in the *Eastern Daily Press*, the *Skegness News* and the *Skegness Standard*.

William Bliss, a clerk from Watford, was on holiday in Skegness on 28 July. He sat in the audience as the rector delivered his customary lecture before entering the lions' cage shortly before 8 pm for the last performance of the day. The cage had a gate at each end, one locked and the other unlocked. Captain Rye was absent for the day but his wife, who held the key to the locked end, was working in the ticket-booth at the main entrance. When Davidson went in to the cage, according to Bliss, the lions were placid but Davidson soon began cracking his whip and shouting to stir them into action. The young lion-tamer Irene Somner described what happened next:

6 Harold Davidson, quoted in the *Skegness News* of 4 August 1937.

When Mr Davidson went in, the lion Freddie was in his way and he tried to slip in between him and the back of the cage. When Mr Davidson tried to get out of the way Freddie reared up on his haunches to get him with his front paws. I got into the cage and tried to beat the lion off, but it dragged Mr Davidson into a corner and we could not move until Freddie dropped him.[7]

William Bliss told the inquest that the rector was carried around the cage 'as a cat does a mouse' for several minutes until the heroic Irene Somner ran in and tried to separate them. Bliss grabbed a broom handle and jammed it into Freddie's mouth but it broke in half. He then picked up an iron bar but could not reach the lion through the bars of the cage. Irene repeatedly hit Freddie on the head with her whip until she managed to prise his jaws apart and Bliss with his bar, together with a second man holding a rake, succeeded in keeping Freddie and Toto (who had stood calmly at the far end of the cage during the attack) both at bay. The crowd scattered in all directions, running for the exits and shouting that the lions were loose and were attacking the rector. Norman Wallace, Davidson's manager, was among them and was seen by a number of witnesses fleeing from the pavilion with his hands above his head and shrieking; although he subsequently told the inquest that he had not fled the scene and had, in fact, tried to help with the rescue.

Davidson, meanwhile, was lying beside the locked right-hand entrance of the cage. Irene shouted over and over for someone to get the key from Mrs Rye who sat, oblivious to what was happening, in the ticket booth. Captain Rye had still not returned, something for which he was heavily criticised at the inquest, and it was some time before the key arrived and the rector could be extracted. Davidson was rushed to the Skegness Cottage Hospital with injuries to his neck, shoulders and back; caused mostly by Freddie's claws, rather than by his teeth. Dr Desmond O'Neill told the inquest that one of the bones in the rector's neck had been broken but, at least initially, his injuries were not regarded as life-threatening.

Late on the evening of the 28th his condition, according to the *Eastern Daily Press*, was 'comfortable' and he was said to have been sitting up in bed while two of his daughters read him the newspaper accounts

7 Irene Somner, quoted in the *Eastern Daily Press*, 2 August 1937.

17 Davidson hosting a pyjama party at the rectory – Estelle Douglas seated right

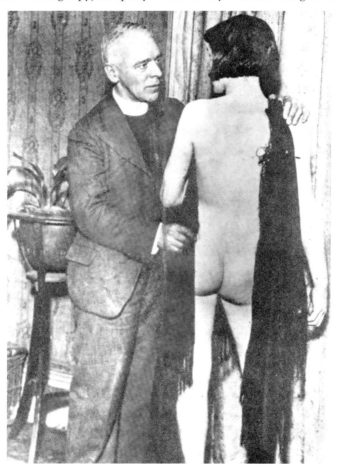

18 Davidson with the nude Estelle Douglas (the line
down the middle is a crease, not a sign of tampering)

19 The rector in the rectory grounds in 1928 with the actress Winifred Wayne, his landlady Flora Osborne and Molly Davidson hiding behind a shrub

20 Letter of support sent by Gerard Gosselin to Major Philip Hamond

REV. H. DAVIDSON M A.
WELL KNOWN AS THE RECTOR OF STIFFKEY,
PHOTOGRAPHED AT THE FAMOUS BARREL EXHIBITION BLACKPOOL 1933.
PHOTO BY SAIDMAN, BROS. BLACKPOOL.

21 Davidson beside his Blackpool barrel, 1933

22 Davidson in Blackpool, c. 1933   23 Posing with the barrel

24 'Beauty and the Beasts' – one of Captain Rye's Skegness animal acts

25 Captain Rye's daughter Betty with a pair of lion cubs

26 One of Captain Rye's animal attractions in Skegness

27 Davidson in the lion's cage at Skegness, summer 1937, just before his death

28 Davidson's funeral in Stiffkey churchyard

29 Davidson's grave in Stiffkey churchyard

30 Captain Rye's act at the Wonderland Theatre in Skegness,
immediately after Davidson's death

of his latest exploits. It also emerged at the inquest that on one day in seven the lions were deprived of food – 'for their digestion' according to Rye and not, as one witness claimed, to make them more fierce. There was also a suggestion, flatly denied by Captain Rye, that Toto was on heat, which might help to explain why the Freddie became so aggressive. Mrs Rye was interviewed for the 1970s BBC radio programme *A Proper Little Gent* and reported that there was another element to the story and, somewhat predictably, it involved young women. She said that on the day the mauling had occurred, Davidson had asked her if could finish early because 'he'd booked two seats at the Arcadia Theatre for two of his friends'. The last show began at 7.30 pm and the rector's two friends – a pair of attractive young women – were standing at the back. Mrs Rye says that instead of concentrating on the lions Davidson kept making eye contact with the two women and waving to them. He stepped back and trod on Toto's tail, causing Freddie to leap up to defend her. Mrs Rye told the programme that as he was being carried out bleeding and injured from the cage he kept asking for his silver-topped ebony walking stick.

There is some confusion over what happened at the hospital. Dr O'Neill informed the inquest that Davidson was diabetic and that the shock of the mauling caused him to fall into a coma. Karilyn Collier, interviewed for *A Proper Little Gent,* said that the rector's oldest daughter Sheilagh had telephoned Molly in Harrow to tell her that he was comatose. Molly immediately rushed to Skegness to be at his side because, she said, she wanted to be the last person to see him before he was put in his coffin. His family categorically denied that he was diabetic[8] and say that the doctors at the Skegness Cottage Hospital, mistakenly thinking that he suffered from the complaint, administered insulin to him. Insulin was then a new drug and its effect on the rector was catastrophic; he fell into an even deeper coma and eventually expired at 1.20 pm on Friday 30 July. The inquest returned a verdict of 'misadventure' – a description that might as easily apply to Davidson's life as to his death.

The villain of the piece, Freddie, was not destroyed after Davidson's death. Only a month after the rector's demise he attacked Joseph

8 Karilyn Collier (*ibid.*) and Colin St Johnston, interview with the author 19 April 2004.

Mellin, one of Captain Rye's trainers. Mellin was foolish enough to put his hand into the cage to stroke the lion's nose, only to have his arm grabbed and pulled through the bars. Freddie released him only after one of Mellin's fellow trainers hit him with a bar and fired a blank shot from a revolver. Mellin sustained a lacerated and broken finger and attempted unsuccessfully to sue Captain Rye for compensation. Freddie remained part of Rye's act and was introduced to the audience as 'the lion that mauled the rector' and, according to Betty Lucas, his party piece was to spray urine over the crowd. Two very sorry credentials. In 1938 he sired a cub called Martin, photographed in the local paper in the arms of Billy Butlin's daughter Shirley. According to the paper the cub's mother rejected it at birth and it was raised by a greyhound bitch.

In death, Harold Davidson attracted more media attention than he could ever have dreamed of during the last few desperate years of his life. The press descended on Skegness *en masse* as soon as news of the attack reached Fleet Street. The wreckage of the rector's life was picked over and analysed and the tone of the reports was overwhelmingly sympathetic. He had achieved iconic status. A report in *Skegness News* encapsulated the mood:

> And what brilliant and jaundiced satirist of human affairs, even with a slightly diseased brain, could have imagined the later career of the unfortunate ex-rector of Stiffkey, passing from one side-show to another, and so to the impossibly bizarre climax in a lion's cage... He was a subject to baffle the psychologist – unless the simple explanation is that his thirst for publicity in almost any form explained most of his actions. Almost his dying words were, 'Am I on the main page?'[9]

Not one to miss an opportunity to make a buck or two, Captain Rye waited only two days before reopening the show and doubling the price of admission. His daughter Mrs Betty Lucas has a photograph of the Wonderland Theatre in Skegness – on the front of it is a sign proclaiming that 'Captain Rye of Skegness Presents the Actual Lion that Mauled

---

9 Collinson Owen, quoted in the *Skegness News* of 4 August 1937. The claims that Harold Davidson's dying words were 'Am I on the front pages?' or 'Am I on the main page?' are almost certainly apocryphal.

and Caused the Death of the Ex Rector of Stiffkey' (see illustration 30). The show was packed but was not without its detractors; Rye told the *Skegness News* that he had received hate mail and an offer of £100 to destroy Freddie the lion. He vowed to continue the show but also promised to provide financial help to the rector's family.[10] Norman Wallace was appalled by Captain Rye's refusal to close the show after the rector's death. Irene Somner, by contrast, was the heroine of the hour. She was inundated with job offers from other menagerie owners, and received at least one proposal of marriage.

The main concern for the family at this point was where to bury the rector. According to the *Skegness Standard* they simply could not afford to move the body to Stiffkey and were considering having him interred in Skegness. Eventually a Peterborough garage owner (presumably with an eye on the publicity) stepped in and offered to convey the body free of charge to Stiffkey.

There is a detailed report of Davidson's funeral in the *Skegness News* of 4 August 1937. He was buried in Stiffkey churchyard on Tuesday 3 August; a day that silenced, at least momentarily, many of his critics. The press, for the last time, were out in force and reported that around 3,000 mourners attended the funeral. Charabancs from far and wide converged on Stiffkey but the carnival atmosphere of the Sunday sermons he gave immediately after the trial was no more and the rector was, at last, accorded the dignity and respect that he had been denied during the last years of his life. He was placed in a plain elm coffin made by F. Wood and Sons of Skegness and made his gratis journey to Stiffkey in the early hours of the morning of his funeral. The then rector of Stiffkey, Harold Fitch, conducted the service and the chief mourners were Molly and four of their children – Sheilagh, Nugent, Patricia and Pamela. His sister Muriel Cox was there, as were the Marquess Townshend, Gladys Marchioness Townshend and members of the Blakeney Branch of the British Legion, of which the rector had once been chaplain. Few of his fellow clergymen had remained loyal but an exception was the Bishop of London, who sent a wreath of white flowers in the shape of a cross, inscribed 'To his old friend, from the Bishop of London'. Among the

10 Captain Rye's daughter Betty Lucas told the author that her father received a letter from Molly Davidson demanding compensation for his death. (Interview on 17 February 2005.)

other wreaths were two garlands of red roses from the rector's two grandchildren, the younger born the day after his death. The church was full of ordinary village folk: fisherman, farmers, cockle gatherers and their families, many of whom Davidson had helped during the twenty-six years he had served as parish priest. At the conclusion of the service four elderly Stiffkey men lifted the coffin and bore it slowly through the gathering of sorrowing villagers to the graveside.

Molly, ever the free spirit, wore a white outfit and shoes; the only signs that she was in mourning were a pair of black shoelaces and a dark hat. Her bitterness over her husband's treatment at the hands of the Church was barely concealed. 'I borrowed ten shillings to buy the hat this morning,' she told a reporter.[11] 'I could not afford any other mourning dress; I am penniless. My husband told me – and the crowds who saw his sideshow at Skegness – that he had begged the Bishop of Norwich to find some way of supporting me and my youngest child. The reply my husband received was "There is no fund available until after your death."'

The *Skegness News* reporter wrote that 'holiday-makers in shorts, beach pyjamas, tennis flannels and hiking costumes flocked to the graveside and scrambled on walls as the coffin was lowered into the grave'. Major Hamond's son Richard Hamond[12] supplied some of the lesser-known details of Harold Davidson's interment. There were people on the church roof, on the roof of the adjacent school and in the trees that surrounded the churchyard. There were people balanced on top of gravestones for a better view of the funeral and the crowd even stripped the leaves from the ivy on the rectory wall right up to the first floor windows for keepsakes. Perhaps the strangest story of all was that when the service was over and it was time to fill in the grave, it was discovered that souvenir-hunters had carried off all the soil and there was nothing left with which to lay the unfortunate rector to rest. Two men were hurriedly sent off to the local quarry to fetch some more. Haydn Cox was taken to the funeral as a small boy and remembers looking down into the open grave and seeing that it had been lined with sweet peas.[13]

11 Reported in the *Skegness News* 4 August 1937.
12 Interview with the author 4 October 2003.
13 Letter from Haydn Cox to the Revd John Penny 26 February 2004.

Most of Davidson's parishioners have now joined him in Stiffkey's churchyard but, despite the passage of seventy years, he is still a part of the fabric of the village. Fresh flowers are still placed on the grave of this complex, enigmatic man and the sons and daughters of his former flock often say that, despite his faults, he was the best vicar the village ever had. People were all too aware of his flaws, but were so fond of him that they quite simply did not care.

10

Was Davidson Guilty?

In his 1934 pamphlet *The Reason Why* Harold Davidson refers to himself as 'living dangerously for God', and it seems that this phrase may be central to understanding his character. The fact that he admits, with great pride, to befriending several thousand young girls while steadfastly denying any impropriety with any of them suggests that he was either a monumental hypocrite or that he was innocent. In these cynical times it is hard to imagine that Davidson's claim could be credible, but this was a more innocent age. It is a self-evident truth that there was plenty of marital infidelity and almost every other imaginable form of sexual hanky-panky during the early twentieth century but there were also millions of people who led blameless, monogamous lives.

By today's standards Davidson might seem to be either thoroughly guilty or at least hopelessly naive. But naivety is not a crime in itself, and when the facts are analysed in a careful, dispassionate manner it is hard to escape the conclusion that he was utterly and publicly disgraced on the basis of very little hard evidence at all. Harold Davidson may, on occasions, have been a fool but he was no rapist. Ned Hamond grew up with the affair and his father Major Philip Hamond was for all intents and purposes, as the author of the original complaint, the agent of Davidson's destruction. If anyone should be convinced of Davidson's guilt you might think it would be Ned Hamond but he says that, in his view, Davidson was innocent and was the victim of dark forces operating within the Church. 'He was a *looker*, not a *doer*,' was Ned Hamond's assessment.

Of the many people who have expressed opinions about Harold Davidson over the past seventy years, the views of Harry Thompson have been some of the most insightful. Thompson made a study of Davidson's character over many years, and when he was interviewed for *A Proper Little Gent* he said that the basis of the rector's success in winning the trust of hundreds of young women was that he provided a 'port in a storm' and convinced them that there was hope for something better in their lives:

> If a young woman pops out of a Tube train and comes out into a rainy, cold London evening without tuppence in her purse, she doesn't want a tract, what she does need is a bacon sandwich and a cup of tea, somewhere to go, somewhere to be, and up to you comes a dapper little chap who looks like everybody's uncle, a sixpenny cigar, a homburg hat, a wing collar. He's very polite, very approachable, quite affable, and he talks to you about the cinema. And his talk about the cinema is all the more convincing because, good heavens, he looks like Charlie Chaplin. He has Charlie Chaplin's gentility, he has Charlie Chaplin's acute human sympathy and you begin to hope, just a little, that after all the streets of London *are* paved with gold, and you may have found a bit of it wearing a homburg hat and smoking a sixpenny cigar.[1]

Thompson clearly believed that there was no real case against the rector. The Church was angered that the eccentric, idiosyncratic Davidson would never conform to their expectations of how a priest should behave and so decided to take action against him; they were effectively 'trying a giraffe for not being an elephant', said Thompson. He added that the real cause of the Church's resentment towards Davidson was that they believed him to be guilty and despised themselves for allowing him to enter the clergy:

'The Church had let him in. And this is an added bitterness against all relapsed colleagues. They make you look silly don't they? It's like a fire brigade which recruits an arsonist.'

Thompson also said that Davidson simply could not help himself, whatever the possible consequences, when he saw a woman whom he thought was in need of saving: 'He inherits the Victorians' love of rescuing people. The Victorians loved rescuing people...if a Victorian lady stopped in the street to straighten her glove she was saved by Gladstone.'

A recurring impression in this affair is that Davidson was a man of possibly unparalleled hyperactivity. In the twenty-five years or so

---

1 Harry Thompson, interviewed for the 1970s BBC radio programme *A Proper Little Gent*.

between the commencement of his weekday activities in London just before the Great War and his death in 1937, he does not seem to have drawn breath. Harry Thompson said that it was significant that Davidson's one great success on the stage was as Charley's Aunt. Charley's Aunt never stops running, is never still; just like the rector himself. Even if we take into account only those events described during the trial, in the newspapers and in other correspondence, Harold Davidson appears to have slept very little (he was clearly an insomniac), to have never remained on the same spot for more than a few minutes and to have crossed paths with literally thousands of people. The Davidson affair is a vortex of plots, sub-plots, names and places – all swirling around one of the most intriguing and complex individuals of recent history.

Davidson seems to have suffered from an almost complete lack of judgement – as evidenced by impossibly ill-conceived excursions to Paris with his teenage wards, and his acquiescence in the Estelle Douglas photo incident on the very day before his trial was due to start. His financial affairs were a disaster area and his problems were compounded by a consuming ego and an unassailable reluctance to take advice from anyone, including his own family. Also witness his behaviour with Kathleen Grant – it is highly significant that she was a respectable Stiffkey girl and yet he was still incapable of avoiding the appearance of wrongdoing. For these reasons alone it is clear that he was entirely unsuited to a small rural parish, and even today his behaviour would probably lead to expulsion from the Church. In Rupert Furneaux's book *Great Issues in Private Courts* there is a chapter on the Davidson affair. Furneaux says, and it is difficult to disagree with him, that the rector was reckless beyond belief: 'he took appalling risks of being misunderstood, he flouted convention and he defied the canons of clerical decorum.'

There may have been a distinct paucity of evidence in this case but the standard of proof was lower than that for a criminal trial. At Archdeacon Wakeford's appeal in 1921 the Lord Chancellor, the Earl of Birkenhead, directed that the same standard of proof should apply in an ecclesiastical court as in a criminal court:

> He is not charged with any offence against the ordinary criminal law, but with an offence against the laws ecclesiastical, being an offence against morality, and upon that charge has been

prosecuted. He is entitled that such an offence shall be proved against him as clearly as if he were subject to prosecution in the ordinary criminal court, and he has to be convicted, if at all, not on grounds of suspicion, but only upon such proof as if the charge were an offence against the criminal law.[2]

North must have been mindful of Lord Birkenhead's words – the Wakeford case had occurred only a decade before and it bore great similarities to this case – yet he draws conclusions and makes inferences that in some instances defy logic and would never have stood up in a criminal trial. Barbara Harris was a calm, effective witness and some of the rector's own courtroom antics did little to help his cause. Nevertheless, there are a number of questionable, even sinister, elements to the case that cannot be ignored. Chancellor North's judgment at the conclusion of the trial is preserved in full in the Norfolk Record Office. His judgment is damning, yet his summing up is a triumph of supposition – he jumped to conclusions that were not supported by the facts of the case and he allowed himself to be influenced by his personal dislike of the rector.

We will probably never know whether Bishop Pollock and Chancellor North colluded to get Davidson convicted but they were certainly friends: they were at university together and North was godfather to Pollock's daughter. In his *I Accuse* pamphlet Davidson quotes Sir Ernest Wild, the late Recorder of London, as saying that if the case had come before him for trial he would have dismissed it in a few hours. It is hard to disagree with this conclusion and it is also difficult to condone the crass methods employed by the prosecution.

When the Bishop of Norwich decided at the beginning of 1932 that Davidson was unfit to be a priest, a single charge or an unobtrusive campaign to get him to resign would surely have achieved the same result. The *Church Times* article of 15 July 1932 was correct: Harold Davidson could have been charged with a single count of immorality and defrocked, and the theatricality of both the trial and the deprivation ceremony in Norwich Cathedral were unnecessary and vindictive. Instead of a quiet expulsion from the Church the book was well and

2 The Lord Chancellor, the Earl of Birkenhead, in 1921. Quoted in Rupert Furneaux, *Great Issues in Private Courts*, London: William Kimber, 1964.

truly thrown at him. Furthermore, the methods employed by the bishop's investigators were heavy-handed, insidious and probably unnecessary. There was never an intention to level criminal charges against the rector and the Church authorities could have achieved their desired aim – to get him to resign – by other means. In *The Age of Illusion*, his commentary on the pivotal events of the interwar years, Ronald Blythe says that by going after Davidson in such a ham-fisted manner both Church and State made complete fools of themselves:

> When human conduct reaches a certain point the ordinary laws cannot apply. Where one insists on applying them there is set in motion a comic process in which retribution slips on its own banana skin, as it were. For Church and State to conspire together so elaborately to exact a penalty from the Rector was a hopeless gesture from the very beginning. That much is plain now. They might as well have tried to lasso a Chagall cow and drag it from its pasture among the stars.[3]

There is one detail of the trial that should have brought the prosecution's case crashing down and yet the rector's defence team completely failed to pick up on it. During the trial numerous letters between Harold Davidson and Barbara were introduced in evidence. The early ones were businesslike and formal with the rector signing himself 'Your sincere friend and Padre' and Barbara writing respectfully to thank him for his help or to confirm some appointment or other. Barbara's letter of complaint to the Bishop of Norwich, while it was undoubtedly a bombshell, is significant for other reasons. Davidson's counsel entirely failed to notice that the letter appears to be written in a different hand to Barbara's other letters (see illustrations). The handwriting is clearly different: Barbara's signature is not the same and there are indications that her letter was coached. I asked Mr Patrick Cheng, an ex-Hong Kong government forensic handwriting and document examiner, to compare the two letters. Unfortunately, since one was written in cursive and the other printed, he was unable to say conclusively whether they were written in the same hand but the fact remains that they appear to be completely different:

3 Ronald Blythe, *The Age of Illusion: Some Glimpses of Britain Between the Wars, 1919-1940*. Oxford: O.U.P., 1963.

I don't think I can give you any conclusive opinion on the author-ship of the two pieces of handwriting. I have examined the two letters. The letter to Davidson was written cursively and appears to be natural handwriting whereas that to the Bishop was printed, that is, with the letters of the alphabet being unconnected. More-over, whether or not the latter letter represents the natural hand-writing of its writer could not be determined...

Handwriting examination is a like-with-like comparison process... and one could hardly draw any conclusion on the comparison of cursive writing and hand-printed writing. There-fore Barbara Harris could neither be confirmed nor eliminated as being the common author to both letters.[4]

In *The Reason Why* Davidson is clearly suspicious of the circum-stances surrounding Barbara's letter. It was posted on the morning of 9 February and yet the chief inquiry agent, Christopher Searle, called to interview Barbara at her landlady's house on the afternoon of the same day, i.e. before the bishop could possibly have received it. Davidson claims that the inquiry agents evinced no interest in Barbara Harris until Rose Ellis's interview with the *Daily Herald* appeared on 4 Febru-ary, in which she recanted the statements she had made to Pollock's investigators and accused them of bribing her. Pollock's men then inter-viewed Barbara's landlady Mrs Lake (who later appeared for the pros-ecution) on about 6 February, and Barbara herself on 9 February. This does indeed, as Davidson claims, smack of collusion and, perhaps, of a desperate search by the prosecution for a replacement for Rose Ellis as a 'star' witness. Davidson does not dispute that Barbara wrote the letter but believes that the Lakes put her up to writing it. In fact, a detailed examination of the document suggests that Barbara did not write it at all, despite the fact that she gave evidence at the trial that she was the author and stood by its contents. The following details a number of the anomalies:

a) The two letters shown in the illustrations are extracts from letters written only four months apart and yet Barbara's handwriting and signature are demonstrably different.

b) Punctuation: Barbara was a seventeen-year-old with limited

4 Letter to the author dated 12 September 2004.

education and, as one would expect, she pays little more than lip-service to punctuation in her earlier letters. However, the letter to Pollock, while it contains poor grammar and misspellings, is punctuated surprisingly well. She uses commas, brackets, apostrophes and quotation marks to good effect, her pages and paragraphs are numbered neatly and she employs underlining and hyphens for emphasis.

c) Clever use of psychology to sway opinion against the rector. There are some deft touches in the letter to Pollock that seem rather at odds with Barbara's age and education and which suggest that she might have been coached. In the first paragraph she anticipates that attempts would be made to discredit her story: she says that Davidson knew she would write but told her that 'my word would not stand against his'. What this does is to make her role as victim appear more acute and also makes the rector's sin seem all the greater. She adopts a similar tone in the next sentence; suggesting that if the rector is allowed to get away with it he will do the same to other girls in the future. Again, the intention here is to present the rector as a man of such moral turpitude that he must be stopped at all costs.

d) The letter is structured and written in a precise manner that inflicts the maximum injury to Davidson's reputation. Again, it appears that Barbara was coached: he bought her a skirt, blouse, hat and gold watch while his wife was 'starving' at home; he entertained 'paying guests' at the rectory while Barbara and Rose were treated little better than slaves; and he spent an hour trying to kiss Barbara on Armistice morning and missed his train as a result. To the last accusation she twists the knife further by declaring that 'this shows you he neglects his parish'.

An important point about this affair, which was entirely overlooked by the Church authorities during the investigation, was that in spite of his faults Davidson was a tremendous force for good. There is no doubt that literally hundreds of young women were saved from a life of prostitution and poverty by the moral guidance and financial assistance proffered by the rector. He may have suffered from a lack of judgement, he may even have been a serial philanderer, but there is no question that a man who had hitherto offered almost thirty years of unblemished service to the Church was entitled to better treatment.

Harold Davidson probably deserved to be quietly defrocked for his shortcomings as a priest: he was wildly eccentric, financially irresponsible and he *was* neglectful of his parish. On these grounds alone he was probably unsuited to the priesthood, but the evidence of his immorality was weak at best, and non-existent at worst. Beyond Barbara Harris's evidence there is next to nothing on which a conviction could have been obtained. Any half-decent lawyer today would have shredded Barbara's credibility, and the case would have collapsed. Levy was a competent lawyer, with a sincere, unshakeable belief in the rector's innocence, but he made at least four major tactical blunders:

1 Consenting to the case being heard before Chancellor North without assessors.
2 Failing to undermine Barbara's credibility as witness.
3 Failing to spot the different handwriting and signatures in Barbara's letter to the Bishop of Norwich and her earlier correspondence with Davidson.
4 Failing to call Molly Davidson and Rose Ellis as witnesses for the defence.

It is my view that the Church of England owes it to Davidson's family to re-examine this case and, if the evidence of immorality is as flimsy as I have suggested, to make a public statement to the effect that despite his undoubted shortcomings as a clergyman, Harold Davidson was *not* an immoral man. His years of good works and his faithful service to the Church were ignored and the public flogging to which he was subjected between 1932 and 1937 was both unnecessary and unjustified. Perhaps then the 'Prostitutes' Padre' will finally rest in peace.

Loose Ends

WHAT HAPPENED TO THE FAMILY?

A ccording to Davidson's grandson Colin St Johnston, in the long term the family recovered well from the scandal. Within a few months of the rector's death in 1937, the family no longer attracted the attentions of the press. Rival issues such as the rise of Fascism, the Spanish Civil War and Japanese expansionism seem to have displaced them from the principal headlines. During the years to come his children remained close, married successfully, and went on to enjoy successful careers. The youngest son Arnold went to India to work for Shell although, according to St Johnston, this was due to a passion for travel rather than a desire to escape the scandal. Molly's remaining years were marred by ill health and she lived quietly until her death in 1955 in a Dulwich nursing home; deaf, blind and cared for by nuns.

In the short term, however, the rector's notoriety caused enormous problems for the whole family. In a letter to his friend and supporter the Bishop of London in February 1934, Davidson described how the scandal had ruined the entire family's prospects:

When I get a letter from my wife, dated 31st January last, in which she speaks of the suffering inflicted on innocent lives, and continues, 'Paddy came in last night, having tramped London to get a job, and the poor darling broke down in sobs. I had difficulty in getting from her what was wrong, and then heartbroken she said, "I can't get a job" – and told me how she had tramped round without food all day to try to get something – with clothes old and worn, hardly befitting for the job she was after. Nothing matters so much as I haven't the money to give her for food, and she has been so run down and weak'…and when I realise that she has been refused over and over again through her name being associated with mine, and even when she has changed her name people have found out who she was…it makes me feel, in spite of my efforts of Christian resignation, that I want to smash somebody myself.[1]

He writes in a similar vein to the Archbishop of Canterbury two years later: 'I wonder if it is possible for you to realise what an appalling thing it is to be pilloried before the world as an immoral man, when I have never had the slightest temptations in that direction… It is monstrous that I should be condemned before the world on the uncorroborated evidence of one street girl.'[2]

Davidson's death on 30 July 1937 left the family destitute. His friends and supporters rallied to help Molly and the children but most were clergymen with limited means and what they were able to offer was not sufficient to provide for the family. The Church was slow to respond to the family's difficulties, despite the fact that they were all entirely innocent of any wrongdoing. There is no doubt that in spite of its rather sententious proclamations that the family should not be penalised for the rector's misbehaviour, that is precisely what happened. Archbishop Lang's papers at Lambeth Palace[3] provide an insight into the true depths of the family's despair. The sequence of documents begins with a letter dated 7 August 1937, a week after the rector's death. It was written to Lang by the Revd W. N. Hallas to draw attention to the family's desperate financial plight. Hallas conceded that 'Davidson's campaign, directed against your Grace …alienated a considerable sympathy which he otherwise would have received from loyal members of the Church of England.' Hallas went on to say that he hoped that Molly would receive financial assistance from the Church despite Davidson's notoriety and that the children be spared further humiliation: 'One hopes at any rate that the children may have their chance in life for apparently their lives have been clouded by reason of the publicity attached to their father's name.'

Archbishop Lang's chaplain and key advisor the Revd Alan Don

---

1 Letter from Harold Davidson to the Bishop of London, 5 February 1934. Paddy was his second daughter and the mother of Karilyn Collier.
2 Letter from Harold Davidson to the Archbishop of Canterbury, 23 November 1936, immediately after the Church Assembly incident.
3 Dr Cosmo Gordon Lang, Archbishop of Canterbury. Papers C17– E7, 1937. Vol. 150, ff 84–91. Held in Lambeth Palace Library.

replied that Lambeth Palace would be unable to provide financial help to the family but suggested that they apply to one of the church charities, such as the Corporation of the Sons of the Clergy or the Poor Clergy Relief Corporation.

Nugent went to Lambeth Palace on 1 November of that year and saw Don. Don's notes of the meeting state that Nugent asked if there was any way in which his mother could be awarded a pension. According to Nugent, Molly was 'living in very reduced circumstances with…practically no means of subsistence other than what is given to her by members of the family'. Don offered to help, albeit more than three months after Davidson's death, by commending an application by the family to one of the Church charities. Don's notes of the meeting include the comment that 'it seems unfair that she [Molly] should be penalised on account of her late husband's eccentricities'.

Nugent applied to both the Corporation of the Sons of the Clergy and to the Poor Clergy Relief Corporation and received grants from both. In a letter to Don dated 3 December 1937, the registrar of the Corporation of the Sons of the Clergy confirmed that a grant had been approved and it is clear from the correspondence that Archbishop Lang had assisted behind the scenes. In his reply to the Corporation's letter Don wrote:

> There is no question that she [Molly] is very hard up and that she has suffered terribly as a result of the eccentricities of her late husband. Whatever view may be taken of his case, it would seem unfair that she should be left to suffer permanently. I mentioned this matter to the Archbishop and he thought that in all the painful circumstances…it would be suitable that a grant should be given.[4]

In Karilyn Collier's account of her grandfather's life she says that the family was devastated by the affair. Her mother's difficulties in securing employment are referred to in Davidson's letter (above) but there was more. She says that her mother even tried changing her name (to Molly's maiden-name of Saurin) but still could not escape the clutches of the press. Eventually the rector managed to get her a job in Belgium

4 Letter from the Revd Alan C. Don to E. Baillie Reynolds, Registrar of the Corporation of the Sons of the Clergy, 3 December 1937.

at the Brussels branch of the 'Three Arts Club', an organisation with which he had been involved before the First World War. The eldest son Nugent, who was already married with a young daughter, had no choice but to remain and weather the storm.

Both Colin St Johnston and Karilyn Collier describe a curious incident that occurred several months after their grandfather's death. A man claiming to be a writer visited the family and told them that he was researching a biography of the rector. Nugent permitted the man to remove most of his father's papers on the condition that he sort them and return them after the book was finished. They were never seen again and the family believes that the Church, specifically the Bishop of Norwich, was responsible. The result, according to Karilyn Collier, was that it 'removed all traces of the rector and any hopes of uncovering the truth behind the scandal'.

Colin St Johnston says that a few of the papers were handed back to Karilyn years later by a distant relative of the bishop and the family believes that the misappropriation of the documents was an attempt to protect Pollock's reputation. Davidson alludes to the subject of Pollock's private life in an extraordinary letter written to the bishop on 23 November 1932. This was among a clutch of letters written by Davidson to the key players in the affair immediately after he had showered the Church Assembly meeting with copies of his *I Accuse* leaflet. He reserved particular scorn for Pollock, the *de facto* architect of most his troubles, effectively calling him a hypocrite.

Davidson claimed in his letter that at the beginning of 1932, when it became clear that he was going to have to fight his case, he was approached by a woman who claimed to have information about Bishop Pollock's private life. She had suggested that the rector employ his own inquiry agents to investigate the bishop and, 'more in a spirit of fun than anything else', he had agreed. His inquiries had turned up no fewer than six separate allegations against the Bishop of Norwich. Davidson, with bitter irony, writes that he did not, of course, believe that the allegations could possibly be true: 'I do not suggest that there was any more truth in the six distinct statements than there was in what Barbara Harris had said about me.' He went on to say that his defence team had actually subpoenaed one of the ladies concerned and she had been present in court during his trial, but in the end they had decided against calling her. Was this the tall, mysterious woman dressed in a vivid scarlet costume and a black hat (see p. 42), who was remarked upon by a reporter from the *Star* newspaper on the first day of the trial? Davidson claims in his letter that if he had divulged what he had known about Pollock it would have destroyed the bishop's career. He had never told a soul, he declared...well not quite: 'The most I have ever said with regard to all this, and that only quite privately, is that a man who has that sort of thing said about him is the last person who ought to have sponsored such an action as was brought against me.'

The whole letter has a rather desperate air about it but there was a sting in its tail. After repeatedly telling Pollock that he would never reveal what he knows about his private life, he goes on to shop him anyway with the following postscript: 'P.S. I have sent a copy of this letter together with a copy of my covering letter to Mr Dashwood, to the Archbishop of Canterbury and the Bishop of London.'

WHAT HAPPENED TO BARBARA HARRIS?

After the trial concluded, Barbara Harris seems to have disappeared without a trace. During research for the 1994 BBC TV programme *Matter of Fact*, notices were placed in various newspapers in the hope that information about Barbara's life after the trial could be obtained. Nothing was discovered and the programme itself failed to induce anyone that knew her to come forward. The only reference to Barbara that I could discover after the trial was in a letter sent by Harold Davidson to the Bishop of London in 1934.[5] In it he complains that Dashwood had secured a job for her at Selfridges under the name of 'Babs Simpson' while his own daughter Patricia had been refused employment again and again because of who her father was.

There is a service called Traceline, offered by the General Register Office of the Office for National Statistics, and during the research for this book I requested a search for Barbara Harris. Despite locating the birth certificates of both Barbara and her sister Sylvia, there is no record of her marrying in England or Wales between 1932 and 1945 and no record of her death in the past twenty years. I also searched for a 'Babs', Gwendoline or Barbara Simpson with similar results. A detailed headcount, or

---

5 Letter from Harold Davidson to the Bishop of London, 5 February 1934. Selfridges' personnel records do not, alas, go back as far as 1934.

National Registration, was conducted in Britain just after war broke out in 1939. There is no record of her in the 1939 headcount either and the most likely explanation for her disappearance after 1932 was either that she changed her name or, alternatively, that she emigrated. Either outcome would hardly be surprising given the notoriety of the case.

I had more success with Sylvia Harris. She and fiancé Percy Malyon did get married, and their slightly unusual surname made the family relatively easy to trace. I interviewed Sylvia's daughter, Mrs Ann Paxman, in October 2003 and discovered a little of what had happened after the trial. The mother of Sylvia and Barbara was mentioned in the trial and had been an inmate in a mental hospital in Eastbourne – she subsequently moved to Norfolk and Sylvia lost touch with her for years.

Sylvia died in 1985 and Ann Paxman told me that she had talked relatively little about the Davidson affair. The experience was so unpleasant and traumatic that she tried to blot it out, she says. What she did say was that Sylvia and Barbara became completely estranged after the trial and lost contact. As far as Ann knows they never saw each other again and the family have no idea what became of Barbara. Sylvia described to Ann an incident during the trial in which she and Barbara were chased through Westminster Abbey by a pack of reporters. She retained a lifelong dislike for journalists and, during the remainder of her life, never made contact with anyone researching the story or otherwise connected with the case. Her mother told her that on one occasion she had seen the BBC presenter Cliff Michelmore doing a 'Where are they now?' slot on TV and suddenly saw her own photograph appear on the screen. Ann told me that her mother thoroughly disapproved of Barbara's lifestyle and had tried repeatedly to get her back on the straight and narrow. More significantly, she also completely disapproved of Davidson and his relationship with Barbara; her mother's words were that 'he was as guilty as sin'. Ann interpreted her mother's remarks to mean that they definitely were having an affair but after so many years and with so many different agendas at work here, her words must be treated with caution.

INCIDENTALS

The first line of Harold Davidson's entry in the *Oxford Dictionary of National Biography* reads: 'Davidson, Harold Francis (1875–1937),

Church of England clergyman and circus performer.' It hardly does him justice. Perhaps something along the lines of 'clergyman, circus performer, champion chess-player, actor, raconteur, rescuer of fallen women, husband, father, friend to the poor, social campaigner, radical socialist, world-class eccentric, insomniac and Great War veteran' might go some way to encapsulating the life of one of the twentieth century's more remarkable characters.

In *English History, 1914–1945* A. J. P. Taylor described the Davidson affair as 'the greatest sensation of the decade': 'Davidson offered a parable of the age. He attracted more attention while he lived than, say, Cosmo Gordon Lang, Archbishop of Canterbury. Which man deserves a greater place in the history books?'[6]

In the seventy years since he died Harold Davidson has, in some quarters, attained a near-mythical status. So many stories have sprung up around him that it is often difficult to separate fact from fiction. So extraordinary and so full was his life that some of the more outlandish tales are actually true while some, quite plausible at first glance, are the invention of the press and others. Among the best known of these tales are that he performed with a dead whale (*true*); that his last words were 'Am I on the front pages?' (*probably false*); and that he once held the world endurance record for sitting on a pole[7] (*almost certainly false*).

Major Philip Hamond's son Richard still lives at Scaldbeck and vividly recalls his parents' anecdotes about the affair. His friend Roger North was Chancellor North's son. Roger assisted his father at Davidson's trial and described Davidson to Richard Hamond as a 'frustrated heterosexual'. Richard thinks this means either that the rector's wife was frigid or that he was impotent. Richard said his parents had told him of other incidents involving Davidson that did not emerge during the trial. They are virtually impossible to corroborate after so many years and the reader should be reminded that Richard's father, Major Philip Hamond, loathed the rector with a passion. One story was that Davidson used to take his current inamorata out to Morston Point on a Sunday morning to frolic in the sand dunes while the bells were ringing

6 A. J. P. Taylor, *English History, 1914–1945*, Oxford University Press, 1965.
7 Letter from Lord Walsingham, Major Philip Hamond's godson, to the *Daily Telegraph*, 17 April 2002.

for the morning service. Things got so bad, Major Hamond said, that he (Hamond) was forced to make an arrangement with Mr Phillips, rector of Bale, to take the service at short notice if Davidson failed to show up. Davidson would often rush in near the end of the service and take over from Phillips, protesting loudly that he was not late.

The second anecdote concerns the unmarried, middle-aged house-keeper of the somewhat crusty, eighty-five-year-old vicar of Bircham Newton, a small neighbouring village. Apparently the housekeeper had offered herself, body and soul, to Harold Davidson and an arrange-ment was made for an assignation the following Sunday at the Stiffkey vicarage. She asked her employer for the day off but the old man wanted the poor, frustrated woman to prepare his Sunday lunch and refused. On Saturday night she put a hundred aspirins in his soup, he was unconscious until Tuesday and she went off for her tryst with Davidson.

The third story, again almost impossible to substantiate after all these years, concerned a plot to steal Morston church's silver Commu-nion chalice, made in 1578 and immensely valuable. Major Hamond told his son that he had got wind of a plan of Davidson's to pinch the cup, presumably to pay off some of the debts with which he was known to have been burdened at the time of his trial. The plot was foiled with the help of his fellow churchwarden, Annie Dickerson, who locked up the church silver in her house.

Davidson sued over one of the many ditties that were written about his exploits but the wags of the day were undeterred. I have unearthed another amusing bit of doggerel about the Stiffkey affair, apparently written by one of his parishioners:

> Bad as ever he could be
> Was the Reverend Harold D.
> Immorality and sin
> Were the things he gloried in.
> Girls of virtue turned and ran
> When his funny stuff began.

> Many years our reverend friend
> Drew the generous stipend;
> Spent it freely, and what's more,

Did his best to borrow more.
Till at last on charges vile
Harold had to stand his trial.

Stripped of garb ecclesiastic,
Harold tried a stunt fantastic.
Clad in Gandhi-like apparel
He paraded in a barrel
Down at Blackpool by the Sea,
Raking in the l/s/d.

Fools and imbeciles were willing
To pay sixpence or a shilling,
Just to say that they'd been blessed
By a priest who'd been undressed.
Finding business growing slack
Harold tried another tack.

Bold as brass, the holy sage
Walked into the lion's cage.
Wallace opening his eyes
Noticed Harold with surprise,
Thought 'Young Albert made me spew
Wonder what this chap will do.'

'Well let's try' then – Scrunch – Oh Lor!
Reverend Harold was no more.

(Verse 1 of 'The Three Harolds' by an anonymous parishioner, written around 1945. The author goes on to caricature the next two vicars of Stiffkey, each of them called Harold, and seems to have been fairly unimpressed with them as well. 'Wallace' and 'Albert' are references to Marriott Edgar's classic 1933 poem 'Albert and the Lion', made famous by the comedian Stanley Holloway.)

There is another ditty in Tom Cullen's book *The Prostitutes' Padre*:

The lock on my door
Has a very stiff key,
And a barrel of oil
Will not let it go free.

When the barrel is empty
We'll all get inside
And pretend we're Little Jimmy
Washed up by the tide.

Harold Davidson was the subject of two musicals, both versions of the same production and both written by David Wright, with lyrics and music by David Wood. The first, called *A Life in Bedrooms*,[8] enjoyed only a short run at the Traverse Theatre, Edinburgh in 1967. The second musical, appearing in 1969, was called *The Stiffkey Scandals of 1932* and starred Terese ('Terri') Stevens as Barbara Harris. Performed at the Queen's Theatre in London, it flopped after twelve performances, despite being filmed and shown on BBC2 on 29 May 1969. The *Evening Standard* theatre critic Milton Shulman in his review (13 June 1969) described it as, 'about as titillating as a pyjama party at Cheltenham Ladies' College'. The *Sunday Telegraph* reviewer on 15 June 1969 wrote: '… this is a cruel, bitingly ironic story. There is a good play in it, perhaps even a good musical. This, regrettably, is not it.' *The Times* of 14 June 1969 wrote that when the verdict was announced, Charles Lewsen – the actor playing Davidson – 'launched into a thirties tap fantasy with dream-girls in white satin'. The fundamental problem seems to have been that in the Swinging Sixties Davidson's behaviour, if anything, seemed rather restrained.

There is a letter in the Norfolk Record Office from the then rector of Stiffkey, the Revd C. H. D. Cullingford, concerning *The Stiffkey Scandals of 1932*. Addressed to the chairman of the BBC, it expresses outrage on behalf of the parish that 'this trivial musical, which ceased to run after only a few days' had revived the public's fascination with the rector. Cullingford wrote that the curious were flocking to Stiffkey once again and that his parishioners 'will have cause to hate the BBC for many years'. A third musical about the affair, *God Made the Little Red Apple*, was also staged in 1969 by the Manchester Drama Group but it, too, appears to have sunk without trace.

A number of commentators have tried to explain the enduring appeal of the Davidson story. Ray Gosling, who presented *A Proper Little*

8 Davidson stated at his trial, 'As a clergyman, one spends one's whole life in bedrooms.'

Gent, thinks that it stems from our desire to escape, for a moment, from the cares of our troubled world: 'So why can't we leave his soul in peace?... Sometimes, when I look along the row of Sunday papers and the serious ones so full of the world in crisis, I think "Sod you Planet Earth" and buy a *News of the World*.'

As recently as 1999 the National Portrait Gallery held an exhibition of photographs entitled *Faces of the Century*. Various celebrities nominated quintessential twentieth-century figures and the writer and newspaper editor Max Hastings selected Harold Davidson; I believe they exhibited a press shot of him posing with a cigar. In 2000 another devotee of the story, the director Ken Russell, produced a short film about the rector's exploits entitled *Lion's Mouth*. In Russell's film, inspired by the Stiffkey affair, journalist Josephine Heatherington investigates the life and death of one Revd H. Davidson, a vicar who was defrocked after taking too lively an interest in prostitutes. At least two television documentaries have told the rector's tale – a recent short programme and the excellent 1994 BBC programme *Matter of Fact*.

Bibliography

Blythe, Ronald, *The Age of Illusion: Some Glimpses of Britain Between the Wars, 1919–1940*, Oxford University Press, 1963.

Coleridge, John K., *St John the Baptist Church, Stiffkey, Norfolk: A Guide round the Church*, Church pamphlet, 1993.

Collier, Karilyn, *Harold Francis Davidson, Rector of Stiffkey: A Biography of His Life and Trial*, pamphlet, Zevrika Publications, 2004.

Collins, Russ, *The Rector of Stiffkey*, illustrated, Foulis Archive Press, 1994.

Crockford's Clerical Directory, London: Church House Publishing, 1918 edition.

Cullen, Tom, *The Prostitutes' Padre: The Story of the Notorious Rector of Stiffkey*, London: Bodley Head, 1975.

Davidson, Harold, *The Reason Why*, pamphlet, 1934.

Davidson, Harold, *I Accuse*, pamphlet, 1936.

Furneaux, Rupert, *Great Issues in Private Courts*, London: William Kimber, 1964.

Hinde, Thomas, *A Field Guide to the English Country Parson*, London: Heinemann, 1983.

Kennedy-Cox, Reginald, *An Autobiography*, London: Hodder and Stoughton, 1931.

Kime, Winston, *Skeggy!: The Story of an East Coast Town*, Skegness: Seashell Books, 1969.

Kime, Winston, *Skegness in the 1920s and '30s*, Skegness: C. H. Major and Co. Ltd, 1988.

Kime, Winston, *Britain in Old Photographs: Skegness*, Stroud: Sutton Publishing Ltd, 1992.

Kime, Winston, *The Skegness Millennium Book of Old Pictures*, Skegness, 2000.

Lang, Dr Cosmo Gordon (Archbishop of Canterbury), Papers, C17–E7, vol. 150, 1937. Held in Lambeth Palace Library.

National Archives document: ADM 6/444 (Admiralty: Service

Records, Registers, Returns and Certificates, Civil Branch Officers'
Service Records, vol. 6, 1905–1916).

Norfolk Record Office documents:

1 Correspondence and Press cuttings re musical and BBC radio
programme re Davidson scandal, 1969, Ref. PD 492/86.

2 Notebooks of K. J. P. Barraclough, barrister, counsel for the
defence of the Vicar of Stiffkey, 1932. Ref. MC2192, 934X6.

3 Suit Papers, Bishop of Norwich vs. Rev. H. F. Davidson, rector of
Stiffkey, 1932. Ref. DN/ADR 15/8/9.

4 Transcript of judgment, July 1932. Ref. MS4389, 57X2.

Oxford Dictionary of National Biography, Oxford University Press,
2004.

Parris, Matthew, The Great Unfrocked: Two Thousand Years of
Church Scandal, London: Robson Books, 1997.

Sansbury, Ethelreda, An Historical Guide to Norwich Cathedral, Dean
and Chapter of Norwich, 1994.

Sternberg, Joan, Don't Tread on the Butterflies: Memoirs of a Childhood in Heacham and Stiffkey, 1912–1932, Dereham, Norfolk:
Larks Press, 2000.

Taylor, A. J. P. English History, 1914–1945, Oxford University Press,
1965.

Thomas, Elizabeth, Joe Jordan: Guardian of the Marsh, Fakenham,
Norfolk: E. M. Thomas, 2003.

Index

Allman, Mrs, 11
Arnold, Dr Thomas, 1
Arrow, Charles (Detective Agency),
    30
Atkin, Lord, 116, 121
Attlee, Clement, 1st Earl, 2

Bacon, Sir Nathaniel, 10
Banister Court School, Southampton,
    1
Barker, Winifred, 69, 79
Barnett, Revd Samuel, and wife
    Henrietta, 1–2
Barraclough, K. J. P., 34; defence
    counsel, 43ff
Barrie, Sir J. M., 2
Barton, Glynn, 139
Beach, Mrs Betty, 44, 46, 55, 72;
    affair with Davidson alleged, 85–6;
    denied, 93–4; 95, 105, 107
Beach, John, husband of preceding,
    93
Bergner, Elisabeth, 2
Bevan, Mary Jane, 59, 99
Beveridge, William, 1st Baron, 2
Birkenhead, 1st Earl of, 154–5
Blackpool Gazette and Herald,
    article attacking sideshows, 133–4
Bliss, William, 145, 146
Blythe, Ronald, 14, 156
Bolingbroke, C. B., 116, 121
Bostock, Harold, 141
Burn, Dorothy, 47; testifies, 61–2;
    72–3, 106
Butler, Percy, testifies, 70–1
Butlin, (Sir) Billy, 141, 143

Butlin, Shirley, daughter of
    preceding, 148

Cattell, Revd R. H., 102–3
Chapman, Revd Hugh, 17
Cheng, Patrick, 156–7
Churchill, Nellie, 48, 69, 78, 92, 95,
    108, 109
Clarke, G., Davidson's business
    manager, 125–6
Clarke, Gladys, 92
Clergy Discipline Act, 19, 27, 29
Collier, Karilyn (granddaughter), 33,
    87, 139, 147, 161; account of
    family difficulties, 162–3
Cowin, Ted, 117
Cox, Haydn, 150
Cox, Muriel, *see* Davidson
Cranage, Very Revd Dr, 121
Critchlow, Cyril, *Blackpool's Golden
    Mile*, 127
Cullen, Tom, and book *The
    Prostitutes' Padre*, xi, 11, 15, 17,
    20, 26, 27, 29, 43, 50, 54, 75, 89,
    131
Cullingford, Revd C. H. D., 169
Curson, G. R., 11
Czinner, Paul, 2

Darbyshire, Albert, 94
Dashwood, (later Sir) Henry, 29–30,
    35–6, testifies, 60–1; criticised by
    Levy, 73; 77, 121, 137, 164
Davidson, Alice (*née* Hodgskin,
    mother), 1
Davidson, Arnold (son), 11, 160

Davidson, Revd Francis (father), 1, 2

Davidson, Harold, birth, 1;
schooldays, 1–3; acting, 2–3;
Oxford, 3–6; unpunctuality, 3, 4,
15, 25–6, 52, 76, 105, 121, 144;
ordained, 5; marriage, 6; living of
Stiffkey, 7ff; grave, 10–11; work in
East End, 13–14; encounters with
wayward girls, 13ff, 26; showgirls,
14; service in Royal Navy, 14–16;
and wife's infidelity, 16–17;
bankruptcy, 18–19; bad relations
with Philip Hamond, 21–4;
accused under Clergy Discipline
Act, 29; and Rose Ellis 30–2;
letters to Bishop of Norwich, 32–3,
34–5; meeting with Bishop of
Norwich, 35; pamphlet *The
Reason Why* cited, 3, 13, 33, 35,
36, 70, 74, 82–3, 152, 157;
meetings with Dashwood, 36;
media frenzy, 37–8; theatrical
touch to matins and evensong at
Stiffkey, 39; Barbara Harris's letter
to Pollock, 40; trial to be in
London, 41; bicycle without lights
charge, 42; case begins, 42;
charges, 43; court proceedings
43ff; mid-trial church services,
64–5; defence costs worries,
69–70; appeals for funds, 72; in
witness box 74ff; questioned over
Barbara Harris, 79–81; challenges
authenticity of her letter to the
Bishop of Norwich, 82–3; and
Actors' Church Union, 83;
unfamiliarity with word 'buttock',
84–5; quizzed on venereal disease,
85; celebrity status, 92; reputation
defended by witnesses, 93–4;
scenes in Stiffkey church, 101–2,
102–3, 104–5; and verdict, 105–9;
costs awarded against, 108; and
wife's and daughter Patricia's views

on, 109–12; doors locked at
Morston church, 113; friendly
congregation at Stiffkey, 114, 117;
performs at Prince's Cinema,
Wimbledon, 116; appeal refused,
116; assaulted by Major Hamond,
118; sentence pronounced, 121–4;
a climax of adversity, 124–5;
farewell to parishioners, 125; to
Blackpool, 126ff; fasts in barrel,
127–8, 129; prosecuted for
obstruction, 128–9; postcards,
129–30; his pamphlet *I Accuse*,
125, 130, 131, 137, 155, 163;
waning of public sympathy, 132,
133; sues successfully over song,
135; wrongful imprisonment, 136;
disrupts Church Assembly, 137;
incident at Victoria Station, 140–1,
144; Captain Fred Rye and
Skegness booking, 140ff; warrant
for arrest for non-payment of fine,
144; mauled by lion, 146; death,
147; 'misadventure' verdict, 147;
funeral, 149–50; his behaviour
assessed, 152ff; Harris
handwriting issue, 156–8; his
papers removed, 163; doggerel
verse about, 167–9; musicals about
life, 169; and *Faces of the Century*,
170; *Lion's Mouth*, 170

Davidson, Moyra ('Molly', *née*
Saurin, wife), xii, 5; breeds
angoras, 11; attitude to 'lame
dogs', 11; problems over daughter
Pamela, 16; 26; stance over Bishop
of Norwich, 34; 47, 50, 57, 61, 67;
stress of trial, 93, 98; 106;
interview with *Sunday Dispatch*,
109–10; 139; encounter with
husband at St Pancras Station,
139–40; to Skegness, 147; attends
funeral, 149–50; bitterness at
Church's treatment of husband,

150; ill health and death, 160; friends' attempts to help, 161; straitened circumstances, 162

Davidson, Muriel Alice (later Cox, sister), 1, 36, 122, 125, 149

Davidson, Nugent (son), 11, 89; and family's poverty, 94; attends verdict, 105; 149, 162, 163

Davidson, Pamela (daughter, later Nelson-Edwards), 11, 16–17, 36; legitimacy issue raised in court, 47, 77, 87, 149

Davidson, Patricia ('Paddy', daughter), xii, 11, attends verdict, 105; interview with *Sunday Dispatch*, 109, 111, 125, 149; scandal's effect on, 160–1, 164

Davidson, Sheilagh (daughter), 11, 147, 149

Devonshire, Duchess of, 81, 82, 94

Dickerson, Annie, 167

Din, Dixie, 54–5, 69

Doble, Dr Francis, 68–9

Don, Revd A. C., 161–2

Doudemain (sometimes Du Domaine), Ernest, 1, 11, 16

Doudemain, Ted, 18, 24

Douglas, Estelle, 38; crucial photograph of, 87–9, 90–1, 94, 96, 97, 105, 154

Douglas, Mae, 38, 87–8, 89, 91

Edwards, Harold, 17

Ellis, Rose, 17, 30–2; story in *Daily Herald*, 38; 43, 45–6, 48, 56, 61, 63, 66, pseudonym 'Mrs Malone', 67, 68; 70, 73–4, 75, 76, 78, 84, 87, 95, 105–6, 107, 109, 130, 158

Exeter College, Oxford, 3

Fabian Society, 1, 2

Fitch, Revd Harold, 149

Frisco, 'the three-legged boy of Italy', 128

Furneaux, Rupert, *Great Issues in Private Courts*, 154, 155

Gannon, Luke, 127, 128–9, 131; threatened with shutdown of his freak shows, 135; 136

Gidney, Arthur, 24

Gladstone, William Ewart, 11–12

God Made the Little Red Apple, musical, 169

Goebbels, Joseph, 16

Gordon, Arthur John, 17–18, 33, 44, 52, 59, 63, 76, 82, 95, 106, 110, 144

Gosling, Ray, 169–70

Grant, Canon A. R., 121

Grant, Kathleen (*née* Pritchard), 47; testifies, 63–4; 65, 154

Gray-Fisk, Clinton, 118

Green, Lottie, 83, 84

Gregory, J. Maundy, 1, 81

Grey, Colonel, 8, 9, 23, 26,

Grey, Mrs (wife of preceding), 8, 9, 23, 26–7

Groom, Colonel, 9, 113

Hallas, Revd W. N., 161

Hamond, Diana (second wife of Major Philip Hamond), 27

Hamond, Ned, 20, 21–2, 30, 152

Hamond, Major Philip, 6, 20–1, 22–4, 26, 27, 29; testifies, 59; locks Morston church, 113; assaults Davidson, 118; fined, 118; letters of support, 119–20; wife, 137; 152, 166, 167

Hamond, Dr Richard, 20, 24, 90, 118, 119, 150, 165, 166

Harcourt, Revd W., 101

Harris, Barbara, 13, 39–40, 42, 43, 44–6; court appearance, 48–57; 59, 60, 64, 65, 66, 68–9, 70–1, 72, 73, 79–81; and her letter to the Bishop of Norwich, 82–3, 99;

condemned from witness box, 93,
94; and by Levy, 96; truthfulness
applauded by Oliver, 98–9;
believed a truthful witness by
North, 107–8; 130, 138, 155;
handwriting issue, 156–8; 159,
163; whereabouts after trial,
164–5; featured in musical, 169
Harris, Sylvia, 46–7; testifies, 57–8;
59, 85, alleged rape, 86–7; 92,
165; marries Percy Malyon, 165;
disapproval of Davidson, 165
Harrow, Dick, 'the world's fattest
man', 128
Hastings, (Sir) Max, 170
Heath, Graham, 30, 137
Heatherington, Josephine, in *Lion's
Mouth*, 170
Henderson, Joseph, 118
Higgins, Charlie, 135
Hodgskin, Gertrude (aunt), 1
Hodgskin, Mary (aunt), 1
Holt, Phyllis, testifies, 69
Horniman, Annie, 5

Jarvis, John, 21, 27
Jarvis, Norman, 21
Jenkins, Roy (Lord Jenkins of
Hillhead), 12
Jo-Jo, 'the dog-faced man', 128
Jordan, Joe, 8, 9
Jordan, Mrs (landlady), 68
Jordan, Thomas, 8

Kennedy-Cox, Sir Reginald, 4;
quoted, 4–5; 5, 14, 15
King, Humphrey, 41; prosecution
counsel, 43ff

Lake, Mrs Alice, 47; testifies, 64, 65,
66; 83, 99–100, 109, 137–8, 157
Lang, Most Revd Cosmo Gordon,
Archbishop of Canterbury, 137,
161, 164, 166

Levy, Richard, defence counsel, 43ff;
assesses evidence, 72ff; closing
speech, 95–6; thanked by
Davidson, 108–9; his blunders
examined, 159
Lewsen, Charles, 169
Lowe, Violet, 59–60, 95, 105
Lucas, Mrs Betty, 141, 142, 144, 148

Malyon, Percy, 58–9, 165
Mariana, 'the gorilla girl', 128
Mary, HM Queen (wife of King
George V), 14
Matter of Fact, TV documentary, 8,
25, 164, 170
Meadows, Dick, 11
Mellin, Joseph, 147–8
Michelmore, Cliff, 165
Monckton, Walter, KC (later
Viscount Monckton of Brenchley),
prosecution counsel, 43ff; 121
Morgan, Violet ('Sweet Vi'), 27–9
Morston, living of, 6, 7, 10; Hamond
connection, 20, 21; dispute over
grave, 22, 23, 24; afternoon service
at, 65; 102, 103, 104; church
doors locked, 113, 114; and
allegiance of parishioners, 113,
117; inhibition notice on church
door; 116; Davidson demands key
to church, 117; 119; Morston
Point, 123; 166–7
Mottistone, 1st Baron, 135

Nelson-Edwards, George, 17
North, F. Keppel, 40–1; friendship
with Bishop Pollock, 41; presides
over trial, 43ff; and Davidson's glib
answers, 75–6, 76–7; sceptical
about Davidson's behaviour, 78;
untutored in ways of the world,
89–90; delivers verdict, 105–8;
criticised by *Church Times*, 115;
121, 124, 137, 139, 155, 159, 166

North, Roger (son of preceding), 89–90, 166

Oldroyd, J. P., 132
Oliver, Roland, KC (later Sir), prosecution counsel, 43ff; cross-examination of Davidson, 81ff; closing speech, 97–100
Olivier, Laurence (later Baron), 2
O'Neill, Dr Desmond, 146, 147
Osborne, Mrs Flora, testifies, 67–8; 75; sues for unpaid rent, 132
Owen, Collinson, 148

Paget-Cooke, Grace (Lady), 55
Parsloe, Billy, 31, 63, 66
Paxman, Mrs Ann, Sylvia Harris's daughter, 165
Penny, Revd John, 150
Perrin, Rt Revd William, Bishop of Willesden, 83
Phillips, Revd Mr, rector of Bale, 167
Pilkington, Mrs Lily, 131
Polanowski, Madame, 'the bearded lady of Russia', 128
Pollock, Rt Revd Bertram, Bishop of Norwich, 27–9, 32–3; falters over prosecution, 36–7; restraining orders against newspapers, 38; 39–40; relationship with Chancellor North, 40–1; 56, 66, and costs of prosecution, 70; 99, 102, 103, 104, 108; no bar on Davidson's preaching, 113; signs notice of inhibition, 116–17; 121, 122; delivers sentence on Davidson, 123–4; 125, 137, 138, 150, 155–6, 157, 158, 159, 163; private life, 163–4
Powell, Revd Edward, 29
Prager, Les, 128
Price Mr and Mrs, 83, 84
Prior, Charles, 68
Pritchard, Miss, see Grant

Quartermaine, Leon, 2

Radcliffe, Revd H. S., 101, 102, 103
Reynolds, E. Baillie, 162
Richardson, Ryder, defence counsel, 43ff; examines Davidson, 74ff
Russell, Ken, Lion's Mouth, 170
Ryder, Joan (later Pollock), 29
Rye, 'Captain' Fred, 141–2, 143, 144, 145, 146, 147, 148; star billing for lion, 148–9
Rye, Mrs, wife of preceding, 144, 145, 146, 147

St Johnston, Colin, 2, 21, 33, 36, 116, 139, 147, 160, 163
St Martin-in-the-Fields, 6
Sales, J. Rowland, xi–xii, 11, 75, 89, 107
Searle, Christopher, 30–1, 56, 66; testifies, 70; 88, 137, 157
Short, Miss ('Miss S'), 66–7
Shulman, Milton, 169
Skegness, expansion of, 143–4
Skerry, Susan (née Jarvis), 21
Somner, Irene Violet, 'La Rena', 140–1, 145–6, 149
Sternberg, Joan, 25–6, 132
Stevens, Frederick, 62–3
Stevens, Terri, 169
Stevenson, Robert Louis, 10
Stiffkey Scandals of 1932, The, 169
Stiffkey village, 7–11, 21–7 passim, 38–9, 101–4, 114; loyalty to Davidson of parishioners, 117; his farewell to them, 125; parishioners addressed in grounds of rectory, 129; Davidson's funeral at, 149–50; grave still tended, 151; attracts the curious, 169
Susi, 'the girl with the elephant skin', 128
Sutherst, Gladys, later Marchioness Townshend, q.v.

Sutherst, Thomas, 6, 7

Taylor, A. J. P., *English History, 1914–1945*, 42, 166
Taylor, Miss, 51, 107, 108
Thole, Inglebert, testifies, 70,
Thomas, Elizabeth, 8
Thompson, Harry, 152–4
Tomlin, Lord, 121
Toynbee Hall, 1–2
Townshend, 6th Marquess, 6–7; wife Gladys, 6, 7, 149
Townshend family, 6
Tuck, Alan, 19, 24–5

Waechter, Evelyn (Lady), 55, 72, 94–5
Wakeford, Archdeacon John, 38, 154–5
Wallace, Norman, Davidson's manager, 142, 144, 146
Walton, Mrs Jessie, 73–4; testifies, 91–2; accused of fabricating evidence, 93; family members, 93; 99, 118
Wayne, Winifred, 67, 75
Whitgift School, Croydon, 1, 2
Wilberforce, Revd Basil, 3
Wild, Sir Ernest, 155
Williams, Miss, 95, 105
Winnington-Ingram, Rt Revd Arthur, Bishop of London, 36, 92, 149; Davidson's letter to, 160–1; 164
Winterbottom, Daisy, 127
Wood, David, *A Life in Bedrooms*, 169
Wood, Derwent, 27
Woodford, Mrs Ada, 63
Wordingham, Sam, 9
Wright, David, *A Life in Bedrooms*, 169
Wright, Lord, 121

Yanika, 'the bird-faced man', 128